Fight for Liberty and Freedom

The origins of Australian Aboriginal activism

John Maynard

Aboriginal
Studies
Press

First published in 2007
by Aboriginal Studies Press

Aboriginal Studies Press
is the publishing arm of the
Australian Institute of Aboriginal
and Torres Strait Islander Studies.
GPO Box 553, Canberra, ACT 2601
Phone: (61 2) 6246 1183
Fax: (61 2) 6261 4288
Email: asp@aiatsis.gov.au
Web: www.aiatsis.gov.au/aboriginal_studies_press

National Library of Australia
Cataloguing-In-Publication data:

Maynard, John, 1954– .
Fight for liberty and freedom: The origins of
Australian Aboriginal activism.

Bibliography.
Includes index.
ISBN 9780855755508 (pbk.).

1. Maynard, Frederick, 1879–1946. 2. Australian
Aboriginal Progressive Association. 3. Aboriginal
Australians — Politics and government. 4. Aboriginal
Australians — History — 20th century. 5. Political
activists — Australia. 6. Aboriginal Australians
— Civil rights. 7. Aboriginal Australians — Legal
status, laws, etc. I. Title.

323.119915

Index by Barry Howarth
Printed in Australia by Pirion Pty Ltd

Cover illustrations: Aboriginal flag taken from The
Long March for Justice and Hope, Invasion Day,
La Perouse, 1998, photo courtesy of Juno Gemes;
Australian Aboriginal Progressive Association shield.

The Aboriginal nation, as a nation of the spirit ... a nation without land or hope, a nation of underprivilege, has existed, probably, from about a generation after Captain Cook landed. Occasionally you meet one of its patriots, one of those people, who, whatever their intermediate likes and loyalties, can be seen to cast their ultimate sympathy, the core of their feelings with this Aboriginal nation ... one does not meet many Aboriginal patriots because it takes a special kind of vision to be one. And it takes courage.

Kevin Gilbert

Foreword

This is one of the most important Australian history books in the past eighty years!

John Maynard has rewritten our understanding of the early history of the modern Aboriginal political movement, and in doing so has made a significant contribution to Australian history. This work is one of the most important history research projects of the past eighty years, in that John has demolished the long-held argument that early Indigenous political organisations were influenced by non-Indigenous Christian and humanitarian groups, and he has shown Indigenous leaders in the first part of the twentieth century were in fact much more politically sophisticated than had been previously thought.

His research shows the strong influence of Marcus Garvey, the 'father of Black Nationalism', on certain Indigenous Australian political activists, and highlights the way in which Garvey's ideas were adopted and adapted to Australian conditions by Fred Maynard and others. This aspect of his book reveals previously unknown associations between Indigenous activists and African–American political groups as early as 1907, when world-famous African–American boxer Jack Johnson met Fred Maynard and others. This was one year before Johnson returned to the Sydney Stadium and (literally) beat Tommy Burns in one off the most famous boxing matches in history.

The stories revealed in John's book are truly remarkable, and emerge from a man whose path in life has a striking similarity to my own. We both came to formal academic studies late in life (each in our mid-forties), both studied history, and both have subsequently challenged the conventional wisdom of academic history by attempting to introduce an Indigenous voice and perspective.

This book confirms why that Indigenous perspective and voice is so important. The story John tells has been waiting to be told since the 1920s, yet several generations of Australian academic historians had either ignored it, or not appreciated its significance. In this way the academy effectively silenced the Indigenous voice and suppressed the story of these events. It is precisely because of non-Indigenous historians' ignorance and/or indifference to the Aboriginal experience of Australian history that we need Indigenous historians like Maynard to give it expression.

Having said that, I would now state that this is a book that should be read by all Australians, as it will enrich their knowledge and further their understanding of the diverse and fascinating network of stories that together make up what we call Australian history.

Gary Foley
August 2007

Contents

Acknowledgments

I am indebted to many people who assisted me with support, guidance and encouragement during the process of researching and writing this work, particularly members of my immediate family: David Maynard, Shirley Maynard, Mary Kondek, Cheryl Oakenfall and all of the extended members of my family. My parents, Mervyn and Judy Maynard, provided me with an inspirational and rich outlook on life full in possibilities.

There are many individuals who also deserve acknowledgement, including Peter Read and Jay Arthur, Heather Goodall, Geoff Gray and Christine Winter, Gordon Briscoe, Tracey Bunda, John Ramsland, John Shipp, Jack and Jean Horner, Reuben Kelly, John Lester, Kevin Ridgeway, Fred Maher, Sharon Cruse, Les Ridgeway, Laurel Williams and Gary Foley for picking up the dinner tab and for his foreword.

My colleagues at Wollotuka, both past and present, all played a part in this work with their friendship, support and camaraderie. There are many Aboriginal communities that I have had the good fortune to work with and within over the course of the past fifteen years; all have offered support, guidance and kindness.

I am indebted to many institutions, including the University of Newcastle, Australian National University, Flinders University, the National Library of Australia, New South Wales State Library, Commonwealth Archives, New South Wales State Archives, Australian Institute of Aboriginal and Torres Strait Islander Studies and the New South Wales Department of Aboriginal Affairs.

I am very fortunate to have received a number of grants during the past several years which have proved vital to my research, and I take the opportunity here to acknowledge their invaluable input. The bodies providing grants include the Australian Research Council, Australian Institute of Aboriginal and Torres Strait Islander Studies, New South

Wales History Council (NSW Premier's Indigenous History Fellowship), Aboriginal History (Stanner Fellowship) and the Australia Council for the Arts.

I dedicate this work to the memory of my grandfather, Fred Maynard, a visionary and Aboriginal patriot who remains a source of inspiration to present and future generations of all Aboriginal people. My cousin, Carol Kendall, was instilled with our grandfather's courage and determination and provided me with much love and passionate interest in my work. Carol so much wanted to see the finished work, and she will remain forever greatly missed by myself, our family and the wider Aboriginal community.

My daughters Candice and Courtney and sons Ganur, Kaiyu and Kirrin-Yurra fill me with much love and hope for the future. Finally, my one true love Vicky has offered and continues to offer so much love, friendship, warmth and intellectual stimulation. I thank you all.

1.
Introduction

The only thing new in the world is the history you don't know.

Harry S Truman

In late 1927 an Aboriginal man wrote an inspiring letter to a young Aboriginal girl abused within the government-operated Aboriginal apprenticeship system. He offered support and encouragement, advising the girl she was but one of many Aboriginal girls suffering sexual abuse within the scheme. He asked for details of those responsible, and promised that he would see the perpetrator in court. Clearly shaken by the girl's experience, his anguish and anger is readily revealed in the text:

> My heart is filled with regret and disgust. First because you were taken down by those who were supposed to be your help and guide through life. What a wicked conception, what a fallacy. Under the so-called pretence and administration of the Board, governmental control etc. I say deliberately. The whole damnable thing has got to stop and by God[s] help it shall, make no mistake. No doubt, they are trying to exterminate the Noble and Ancient Race of sunny Australia. Away with the damnable insulting methods. Give us a hand, stand by your own Native Aboriginal Officers and fight for liberty and freedom for yourself and your children.[1]

The man who wrote that letter was Fred Maynard, and this is his story.

Maynard is one of the great forgotten Aboriginal patriots and an organiser of political activism. He was born, appropriately enough, on Independence Day, 4 July 1879, at Hinton, near Maitland in New South Wales. He was instrumental in forming the first unified and long-lasting politically motivated and organised Aboriginal movement, the Australian Aboriginal Progressive Association (AAPA). He proved to be an exceptional man, an inspiring leader and spokesman, and a compassionate visionary who rose up to defend his people's rights.

Maynard's story is deeply entwined in the tragedy of Aboriginal experience and the origins and early development of organised Aboriginal political activism of the twentieth century. From the outset of European occupation, Aboriginal history has been denigrated and distorted to the level of myth, legend, fable and even fairytale. More recently, writing about the Aboriginal presence has been presented as being completely outside the mainstream Australian historical landscape.

My evaluation of Fred Maynard and the organisation he led, the AAPA, is of critical importance to the revision of Australian Aboriginal history. The AAPA is now rightfully recognised as the precursor of the Aboriginal political movement. Yet for several decades the deeds and struggles of the AAPA were largely ignored, misunderstood, forgotten and hidden, its legacy fading into oblivion.

I unashamedly acknowledge the deep personal significance of the story of Fred Maynard and the AAPA, both from the perspective of an Aboriginal man conveying an Aboriginal viewpoint of Australian history, and because Fred Maynard was my grandfather. I openly declare that the matter is close to my heart; my desire is to see the story told.

Sadly, Fred died eight years before my birth so I never had the opportunity of meeting this remarkable Aboriginal patriot except through documents, photographs and oral memories. The story is of unquestionable importance to my own family as it highlights the high levels of commitment and sacrifices that Fred, his compatriots and their families made in their constant battle to improve Aboriginal conditions at a particularly difficult and challenging time in Aboriginal history.

Opposition to the British invasion of Australia is not some new-found strength and ideology that Aboriginal people have suddenly discovered or stumbled upon. It did not spring from the Mabo decision or the *Native Title Act*, nor was its birth solely a result of the vibrant 1960s, which culminated in the establishment of the famous Aboriginal Tent Embassy in Canberra.

It is true that the 1960s was a time of excitement and turmoil in Australian politics: expansion of the Cold War, the escalation of the divisive war in Vietnam, and confrontation over civil rights for Black America filled the TV screens and airwaves. None of this went unnoticed by Aboriginal people. They marched, protested, spoke out and wrote of the injustices of the past and present. To many people, the period seemed to mark the origins of Black political consciousness in Australia. In 1965 Charles Perkins led the freedom rides through New South Wales, 1966 witnessed the Gurindji walk-off at Wave-Hill, Aboriginal people played a significant part in achieving the overwhelming 'Yes' vote in the 1967 referendum. The establishment of the Aboriginal Tent Embassy on the lawns of Parliament House in 1972 seemed to reaffirm the arrival of an organised and united Aboriginal political movement.

There are numerous examples of the influence that international Black politics had on Aboriginal political activism during this period. In 1972, Paul Coe stated:

> Black Power in Australia is a policy of self-assertion, self-identity. It is our policy, at least as far as we in the city are concerned ... to endeavour to encourage Black Culture, the relearning, the reinstating of black culture wherever it is possible ... The Afro-American culture, as far as the majority of blacks in Sydney are concerned, is the answer to a lot of black problems because this is the international culture of the black people.[2]

No less a voice than the incomparable Malcom X perceptively commented on the oppressed position of Aboriginal Australians in 1965:

> The aboriginal Australian isn't even permitted to get into a position where he can make his voice heard in any way, shape or form. But I don't think that situation will last much longer.[3]

However, it is obvious that Malcom X had no comprehension or knowledge that an Aboriginal political voice had been active, constant and outspoken against prejudice and oppression for decades, and that there had been a substantial and sustained international Black influence in that process. He went on to say:

> Just as racism has become an international thing, the fight against it is also becoming international. Those who were the victims of it and were kept apart from each other are beginning to compare notes. They are beginning to find that it doesn't stem from their country alone. It is international. We intend to fight it internationally.[4]

What Malcom X was proposing was not in fact something new; rather, it was more of a united tradition of opposition by oppressed groups around the world. But this tradition had already existed; its history had largely been forgotten or erased.

Politically, the 1920s and 1930s were as tumultuous and as international in their outlook as the 1960s. Some people may remember William Cooper, Bill Ferguson, Pearl Gibbs and Jack Patten. These eminent Aboriginal freedom fighters were prominent during the late 1930s and instigated the 1938 'Day of Mourning' protest in Sydney during the celebrations of Australia's 150th anniversary of European settlement. Some observers have remarked that Aboriginal protest groups of the Cooper, Ferguson and Patten era were 'neither the most articulate nor the most influential',[5] but this fails to acknowledge the constraints and thinking of their period. The supposed and enforced superiority of the white place in the world was, from a white perspective, unquestioned and unchallenged. It has been observed that Ferguson and Patten actually embraced 'the notion that blacks deserved citizenship and equality via complete absorption into mainstream Australia by assimilation'.[6] Professor Eric Willmot — a noted Aboriginal academic and author — believed that 'this appeared to lead Aborigines in the 1930s and 1940s towards outright rejection of their primary identity'.[7]

Willmot concluded that Ferguson's demands were 'a plea by mixed race Aborigines to be recognised as Europeans'.[8] Geoffrey Stokes, commenting in *The Politics of Australian Identity*, tried to confirm Willmot's analysis when he concluded that 'in the 1930s and 1940s, when they were arguing for full citizenship rights, Aborigines relied on a conception of identity that suppressed notions of Aboriginal difference from Europeans'.[9]

However, these assumptions have overlooked the fact that Aboriginal people during this period had been exposed to high levels of assimilationist propaganda, indoctrination and restrictive policy. The response that Ferguson, Patten, Gibbs, Cooper and their followers instigated was the only option by which they could ensure the survival of Aboriginal peoples and histories, all of which were under attack from restrictive government assimilation policies.

Whether Willmot and Stokes are right or not, I shall show that a decade earlier, with Fred Maynard and the AAPA, such an approach would have been totally unacceptable. Writing about the 1920s political scene, historian and academic Heather Goodall said that:

> The 1920s activists had felt free to make clear assertion of the value and continuation of Aboriginal traditional culture, insisting that they must be recognised as civilised by virtue of *both* 'our more ancient civilisation' and their competence within European culture. The 1930s movement felt no such freedom, and avoided the topic altogether.[10]

Significantly, she went on to remark that:

> the confident and proud public assertions of the value of traditional civilisation which Fred Maynard had been able to make in the 1920s were therefore not to be heard in the 1930s political statements. This made it difficult to argue for any rights to land, which arose from prior possession based on traditional law and continuing traditional affiliation.[11]

It is critical to remember that the 1930s organisation the Aborigines Progressive Association (APA) was a different group entirely to the 1920s AAPA. Extraordinarily, none of the (senior) activists from the 1920s were visible in the late 1930s. Some have argued that the 1930s campaign was fundamentally about civil rights and not so much about Aboriginal rights, particularly in relation to land. Personally, I think they were no less radical, from their demands to be recognised as equal citizens to the pride in identity and Black nationalism, which was the dominant Aboriginal platform twelve years before. However, a clear distinction does need to be made.

Much of the confusion between the politics and climate of the AAPA in the 1920s, and that of the APA in the 1930s and 1940s, is due to a simple lack of research. It was not until 1974, when Jack Horner published his benchmark study of Bill Ferguson and the APA, that any post-war mention at all of the earlier AAPA surfaced. Discussion of the AAPA only came about through the memory of Charlie Leon, an Aboriginal man 'who had left home at Forster in 1920, earning a labourer's living anywhere he could, was working on the Cotter Dam near Canberra in 1926, but two years later was running a vaudeville troupe, "Leon's Entertainers"'.[12] Leon travelled widely with his show and witnessed firsthand discrimination and prejudice. He described to Horner a meeting with Bill Ferguson, during which they discussed the need to establish an Aboriginal political voice. During this meeting Leon told Ferguson about the AAPA, 'led by a "livewire" Aboriginal named Fred Maynard: but nobody heard of it now'.[13] Ferguson responded that he had knowledge of them and that they 'held three annual conferences, but were hounded by the police officer acting for the Protection Board'.

This short acknowledgment was instrumental in establishing a number of incorrect assumptions: firstly that the AAPA ceased operations in 1927, and secondly that the organisation was confined to Sydney. Horner later wrote to me that, at the time he wrote his book, there was little or no readily available information of the AAPA or on Fred Maynard. He had come across only scant information and simply assumed that they had either made little impact, or that no substantial records remained of the organisation.[14]

On the availability of this slight evidence, subsequent academics and historians followed Horner's lead uncritically and concluded that Ferguson and the APA signalled the onset of an organised Aboriginal political agenda. This theory simply rested on the fact that no one had gone back further than the late-1930s organisation or been fortunate enough to uncover substantive material to argue against the theory. This changed in

1982 when Heather Goodall produced her doctoral thesis 'A history of Aboriginal communities in NSW 1909–39', and her subsequent book, *Invasion to Embassy.*

Goodall discovered material relating to the AAPA, most notably letters and petitions written by Fred Maynard to the New South Wales State Government and the New South Wales Aborigines Protection Board. The most important discovery was in a Newcastle newspaper, *The Voice of the North*, edited by John J Moloney — a fierce nationalist. To his credit, Moloney gave Aboriginal leaders such as Maynard and Tom Lacey editorial space and concerted press coverage and support. Goodall's findings established that the AAPA was much more than some small Sydney-centred organisation. Her work uncovered information on the make-up of the organisation and its platform, one which centred on land rights, citizenship, protection of Aboriginal culture, called for a royal commission into Aboriginal affairs, and a concerted attempt to end the practice of removing Aboriginal children from their families.

The onset of organised Aboriginal political agitation in 1924 had seen Aborigines publicly voicing dissatisfaction about their treatment by white Australia through street rallies, meetings and conferences. The AAPA initiated a concerted and united Aboriginal front, bringing it to the notice of the media and the wider public for the first time.

Importantly, the organisation had studied the international racial situation in Africa, the United States and in other parts of the globe, and used its knowledge of world events to its advantage. The AAPA proved to be a revelation and an inspiration to Aborigines. They petitioned at all political levels: the radical Labor State Premier of New South Wales, Jack Lang; the conservative Prime Minister, Stanley Bruce; the Governor General, Baron Stonehaven; one member even had the audacity to send correspondence as a formal petition to Buckingham Palace beseeching King George V to intervene in the treatment of Aboriginal people.[15]

The measure of the AAPA's success at generating knowledge and interest among Aboriginal communities and across considerable distances can be measured by comparing attendance levels at meetings. In 1939 the western branch of the APA attracted sixty Murris to its second annual general meeting in Dubbo;[16] the 1938 'Day of Mourning' protest in Sydney attracted 100 people;[17] and the coastal faction of the APA led by Jack Patten in mid-1938 could boast an active membership of 118 members.[18] In contrast, the AAPA (in 1925, after only six months of operation) had established eleven branches and a membership which exceeded 500 Aboriginal people.[19] The area the AAPA covered included vast regions of New South Wales — from the south coast through Sydney and Newcastle to the mid to far-north coast and west to inland centres such as Angledool. Knowledge of the AAPA's activities received coverage in South Australia and Queensland. The AAPA attracted over 250 Kooris to its first annual general conference in Sydney, and nearly tripled that with several hundred Kooris attending its second conference in Kempsey in 1925.[20]

The AAPA took a carefully organised political stance that had the authorities at a loss at how to deal with such an unexpected and persistent form of agitation. Here was an Aboriginal group that played a supporting role in establishing a hostel at Homebush in Sydney for Aboriginal girls who had run away from white employers after maltreatment. Once knowledge of the Aboriginal support for this home became available to the authorities, Church support for the home was withdrawn and it was subjected to constant police surveillance, interference and threat. The AAPA applied and won the right to be incorporated as a company against the direct opposition of the New South Wales Aborigines Protection Board, which had even sought the advice of a Crown solicitor on how to halt that very process. It was a rare occasion during that time for the Board to feel the heat of the media and public scrutiny.

Fred Maynard, Tom Lacey, Sid Ridgeway, Dick Johnson and the other Aboriginal leaders of the AAPA realised that the institutionalised framework set in place by governments and their agencies was an orchestrated and sinister mechanism supporting an ideology that held horrific implications for Aboriginal Australia. Lacey, Ridgeway and Johnson were close friends and colleagues of Maynard and were influential office bearers of the AAPA. They were well informed, not just of Aboriginal issues but also of national and international awareness and understanding of racial issues. They realised that the whole process was about the complete disintegration of Aboriginal culture and its absorption into white society.[21] In light of the events of the decades that followed, their fears were clearly valid and vindicated.

For white Australians the most unsettling aspect of the AAPA was the fact that it was led by a self-educated and well-educated Aboriginal man with a great command of both the spoken and written word. Maynard spoke and wrote passionately and insightfully about the injustices and atrocities committed against Aboriginal people. He spoke of things that either many white people did not know or were not aware of, or simply did not want to know. The power of the message that Maynard so defiantly expressed some eight decades ago has not been diminished with time, nor can his grasp of the realities of the Aboriginal situation be at all underestimated. Even when read today, his letters and petitions are, in every sense, modern in tone and as relevant as the day he penned them. He declared that Aboriginal people's rights regarding occupation and land ownership over-rode all others. He bluntly refused any notion of inferiority for Aboriginal people. The New South Wales Government and its agencies, which confronted the AAPA and its operations with force and aggression, did not intimidate him. There was a concerted official attempt to stamp out the flickering flame of hope that the AAPA had generated among Aboriginal communities. The methods employed against the AAPA included direct harassment of its office bearers, attempts to discredit their reputations, and a covert bid to encourage division from within the ranks of the AAPA's structure. The attempt to cause division and fracture from within failed, though as a method it has been used against Aboriginal communities and organisations in the decades that followed.

But the AAPA abruptly ceased public operation in 1928. Evidence suggests the AAPA was hounded and harassed out of existence by the New South Wales police, acting on behalf of the Aborigines Protection Board.[22] Indeed, the head of NSW Police was also chair of the Aborigines Protection Board!

Tragically, Maynard was severely injured in what has been reported as a work-related accident. His injuries were so severe that he spent twelve months in and out of hospital. His leg was amputated and, thereafter, he was incapacitated. He endured a prolonged battle with illness from which he never recovered. He died in 1946.

The AAPA was not just the first Aboriginal political movement in Australia, it was also the most contemporary in its philosophy and internationalist in its outlook. Its demands for Aboriginal land for Aboriginal people and for the ending of child removal, and its efforts to enfranchise the Aboriginal population of New South Wales, are as relevant today as they were in the 1920s. But the Goliath in this battle — the New South Wales Aborigines Protection Board — was a determined enemy. In *Fight for Liberty and Freedom* I shall show how the AAPA and its supporters challenged the Board, and the lengths the Board went to defeat its opponent. I shall also reveal the AAPA's links to other Black movements internationally through the Sydney waterfront and the subsequent influential inspiration of that contact on Aboriginal political mobilisation and directive.

2.

Fred Maynard's Early Years

*The person who seeks the connecting threads in the history of his life
has already ... created a coherence in that life ... [which represents]
the root of all historical comprehension ... The power and breadth
of our own lives and the energy with which we reflect on them are
the foundations of historical vision.*

Wilhelm Dilthey

Fred Maynard's childhood and formative years played a significant
role in shaping his future political stance and orientation. As a young
man Maynard travelled widely, witnessing firsthand the hardship and
conditions of his people. These early experiences were significant in
shaping his political agenda and beliefs. Indeed, Maynard's background
is a metaphor for the Aboriginal experience since 1788.

Fred Maynard was born on 4 July 1879 at Hinton, near Maitland,
New South Wales. In that same year JD Woods described the destiny of
Aboriginal people as the white majority saw it:

> Without a history, they have no past; without a religion they have no
> hope; without the habits of forethought and providence, they can have
> no future. Their doom is sealed, and all that the civilised man can do
> ... is to take care that the closing hour shall not be hurried on by want,
> caused by culpable neglect on his part.[1]

These remarks foreshadowed the hurdles and ignorance that Maynard
was forced to endure and battled to overcome in his adult life. Woods's
remarks — that Aboriginal people are a people without a recognised history,
not just in their traditional past but also in the context of the immediate
past — seem incredible now. The terrible impacts of colonisation were
not just in a recent past that was already being orchestrated and obscured.
Both then, and well into the future, these impacts were a daily reality for

Aboriginal people. Only ten years before Woods's declaration and Fred Maynard's birth, an article in the *Newcastle Chronicle* stated categorically:

> We have not only taken possession of the lands of the aboriginal tribes of this colony, and driven them from their territories, but we have also kept up unrelenting hostility towards them, as if they were not worthy of being classed with human beings, but simply regarded as inferior to some of the lower animals of creation.[2]

This was the era and worldview that Fred Maynard was born into and grew up in. One of six children born to Mary Phillips, an Aboriginal girl, and her English labourer husband, William Maynard, Fred's Aboriginal roots lie with the Worimi people of the Port Stephens area immediately to the north of Newcastle. Mary's mother, also named Mary, is recorded as an Aboriginal 'who can read' and was born at Port Stephens.[3]

At the time of Fred's birth the Australian continent had a history recognised by the British that barely encompassed 100 years, yet dispossession of Aboriginal land and disintegration of families was already well entrenched. The experience of Fred, his brothers and sisters pre-empted future government policies of child separation. Although they were not forcibly removed, they lost their mother at an early age and were abandoned by their father. Fred's early life experiences were undoubtedly a major component of the underlying forces that drove him in the future. From his own harsh personal experiences he instinctively sought to oppose government policy towards Aborigines and to try every way possible to instil hope in his people.

Little is known of the life or whereabouts of Fred's grandmother, Mary Phillips. She probably belonged to the Maiangal clan of the Worimi, which centred on the southern side of Port Stephens. This would explain the strong ties Fred kept with the Ridgeway family, evidenced during the later years of his life. Mary Phillips senior was born in 1827, which ties in with the arrival of the Australian Agricultural Company and the schools established in the locality by Lady Parry — the wife of the famed Arctic explorer Sir Edward Parry, commissioner of the AA Company. Mary Phillips probably received her European education through Lady Parry's educational initiatives.

In 1846 Mary married Jean Phillipe (anglicised to John Phillips) at Dungog; she was nineteen and he was thirty-three. Jean Phillipe was from the Isle of France (Mauritius) and was recorded as a settler and farmer. Phillipe was illiterate and, up until his death on 29 January 1875, always signed his name with an 'X'. Family tradition relates that Jean Phillipe was a Black African. It is possible that Phillipe first arrived in the Port Stephens area to gain work with the AA Company.

After their marriage he and Mary moved to nearby Dungog and established a small farm at what was variously called Tee Tree Flat or Croom Park. They had eight children: Isabella, Eliza, John, Mary, Thomas, Robert, Nancy and Caroline. The family continued to occupy the farm until Phillipe's death. By this time their daughter, Mary (Fred's mother), was in the employ of the Pearce family at Hinton, near Maitland, where she worked as a domestic servant at the homestead known as Melville House.

The house still stands today, an imposing building with a historic past.

The original land grant was issued in 1823 to William Hicks, a lieutenant in the Royal Navy. It is thought that Hicks named the property 'Melville' in honour of Viscount Melville, then First Lord of the Admiralty. In 1825 the original dwelling was robbed by bushrangers, who stole provisions, firearms, ammunition and other items of value, including Lieutenant Hicks's watch. The house we see today was commissioned in 1839. It was built entirely by convict labour, and the sandstone used is slightly channelled and sparrow-picked. A plaque above the back door honours the architects with the inscription 'Erected 1839 by F Mitchell, J Curtis Archt'.

Mary Phillips suffered the fate of many Aboriginal girls employed in domestic service when she fell pregnant. However, Mary's younger sister Caroline suffered a similar but more horrifying experience. The *Sydney Morning Herald* of 27 October 1875 reported that 'Caroline Phillips, a coloured girl, was brought before the Court charged with attempting to murder her infant male child on Sunday, the 10th instant'.[4] The report stated that Caroline had been in the employ as a general servant of a Mr Fleming in Park Road, Sydney for about two weeks. On the morning of 10 October Fleming stated that he heard the defendant being sick in the toilet. He ordered her out at once. He stated that he then heard a noise in the toilet and when he looked in discovered a new-born baby. The police were called and Sergeant Bremner later stated that when he arrived he found the defendant lying on a sofa cradling the child. This picture of Caroline on the sofa with the baby in her arms contradicts the image of a young mother accused of attempting to murder her baby. Under questioning, Caroline Phillips acknowledged that the child was hers and a man named George was the father. A Dr Egan attended, and he later stated that he examined both the mother and child. He stated that the mother had 'only recently been confined without having had proper attention'.[5] Caroline Phillips was just fifteen years of age, and one can only hazard a guess at the confusion, fear, shock and horror she was experiencing. With no understanding, compassion or consideration she was sent to the

Benevolent Asylum. Another report on 10 November 1875 highlighted the second Court sitting:

> Caroline Phillips an Aboriginal, was indicted with having on the 10th October, 1875, at Sydney feloniously and unlawfully attempted to strangle with intent to murder, a male infant by tying a piece of calico around its neck. A second count charged the prisoner with having attempted to suffocate the child by casting it into the cesspool of a privy.[6]

Caroline Phillips pleaded not guilty but she was undefended. The jury found her guilty of the first count, but recommended her to mercy. The judge sentenced her to three years' hard labour in Darlinghurst Gaol, the colony's central prison. Her baby was taken from her and no records have thus far revealed of his fate. Caroline did not see out her sentence. She died on 13 April 1876, not even five months into her sentence and aged only sixteen — an early case of an Aboriginal death in custody.

Stories about Mary Phillips hold that the likely culprit and father of her child was Mr Pearce, the master of Melville House. Mary gave birth to her first son, William, on 6 September 1875. To cover his misdemeanour, and still feeling some tug of guilt, Pearce paid an English labourer at the property, William Maynard, to marry Mary. They were married in 1876 and the family was given the use of a small cottage on the property. Mary Maynard proceeded to give birth to five other children: Emily, Emma,

The Pearce family at Melville House in Hinton, c. 1880, the birthplace of Fred Maynard. William Maynard, the firstborn son of Mary Phillips, is the only member of the Maynard pictured, standing third from the right.

Fredrick, Arthur and Florence. She died in 1884 when giving birth to twins, both of whom also died. After Mary's death William Maynard deserted his children. He moved to Maitland and had two further marriages and families with non-Aboriginal women. Of the children he left behind at Hinton, the first-born, William (in reality the offspring of Pearce), was taken in by the Pearce family. Elizabeth Pearce, the spinster sister of Mr Pearce, brought William up as her own son. He went on to be well educated and was taken to Britain for a period. When Elizabeth Pearce died she left the estate to William. However, members of the Pearce family contested the will and the bulk of the estate was eventually returned to them. William married twice and was the only one of the Maynard children to remain in the Maitland area. He remained in the vicinity and on the land until his death.

The other children were not wanted and they were doled out to members of the local community. A Christian minister and his wife at Dungog took in Fred Maynard and his brother, Arthur. The boys were aged five and four, and their journey through young life proved to be a venture at times into hell. The minister raised them with harsh Protestant discipline. Fred later told his children of the horrific experiences inflicted on him and his brother, describing the minister as 'the cruellest man that ever walked the earth'.[7]

The brothers were treated like animals and forced to live in the stable. They did all the tedious jobs around the small dairy attached to the presbytery and took a beating if they did not perform their tasks to perfection. They had to get up and milk the cows before first light. Even at the height of winter they had to go out barefoot into paddocks covered with heavy frost. They had no shoes at all and Fred Maynard recalled that he 'would stop and stand with his feet in the fresh warm cow patties to ease the blinding cold and pain of his feet'. Fred's son, David Maynard, recalled that, 'Dad had a hard life and, when someone has a hard upbringing, it makes them respect other things, other people and makes them more sincere'.

There was some small consolation with their experience, though, as the Minister provided the boys with access to a large library of books and ensured that they learned to read. 'From the time he was eight,' said Fred's daughter, Mary Maynard-Kondek, 'Fred read everything that was placed before him, and by the time he was twelve had educated himself on a wide variety of topics, from philosophy to biology'.[8]

The boys fled the clergyman's harsh clutches sometime in their early teens, but until his death in 1946 Fred still carried an old Scottish dictionary with him wherever he went. He used the dictionary to expand his vocabulary and understanding of the English language, and this book remains to this day as a treasured memento of the Maynard family.

The boys' relatives had kept in touch with them during their young life. Their uncle, Tom Phillips, who lived at St Clair near Singleton, had maintained contact with his nephews, and would prove a source of inspiration and support. Tom was a prominent and highly politicised individual, and one of the few Aboriginal farmers who had settled and farmed St Clair reserve outside Singleton. This reserve was first to suffer the indoctrination of missionaries, then control was taken over by the New South Wales Aborigines Protection Board in 1916 before it was completely swallowed up and closed off to Aboriginal people altogether in 1923. As Indigenous historian James Miller noted:

> Tom Phillips, an uncle of Jack Miller, chose not to accept the white man's religion. During the 1900s Tom Phillips's name was a very significant one in the Singleton and St Clair areas. His name appeared in several editions of the *Singleton Argus* in the 1900s while nothing was said of him in the Inland Mission's journal *Our Aim*. Had Tom Phillips been a Christian, the latter publication would have most certainly written about him.[9]

Fred and his brother probably spent time at St Clair with their uncle before eventually finding their way to Sydney to live with their older sisters Emily and Emma. The later experiences of land loss at St Clair, and the impact of that event on his Uncle Tom, was one of the significant catalysts that triggered Fred's political revolt.

During the years prior to and just after the turn of the twentieth century Fred Maynard worked and travelled extensively. He was a drover and, at one time, operated a nursery in Sydney. He remained an avid and skilled gardener throughout his life. He spent time as a photographer and the Maynard children recall his photographer's tray, which in their childhood years they used as a washing up tray. He had pictures on the wall of timber-getters and bullock teams. These pictures may well date the time he spent on the mid and far-north coast of New South Wales working as a timber-getter. It is ironic that Aboriginal people now sought and found opportunity in the timber industry, as in the past they had suffered horrifically at the hands of white timber-getters.

This period undoubtedly established and reconnected him to other relatives and associates as a large number of Aboriginal men were involved in the industry. Fred's work here at this time would have put him back in contact with the Ridgeway family, as several of the Ridgeway boys were working as timber-getters. William and John Ridgeway 'had been fighting for land against white encroachment at Tea Gardens since the early years of the century'.[10] Despite the obvious success of Aboriginal farming enterprises, white pressure upon these lands began to intensify. John Ridgeway was forced to begin the long and eventually fruitless fight for his reserve land at Forster in 1908. White residential expansion at Forster marked the beginning of a vicious campaign to remove the Aboriginal families from their hard-worked and well-established properties. These white opponents wrote letters to the media and politicians in their attempts to have the Aboriginal families removed. One individual who did not hide his racist sentiments and mentality wrote in the press:

> It is a disgrace to allow these few people to live in the centre of our tourist town and to insist that white folk must put up with them as next door neighbours. They occupy a block embracing the choicest building lots in the town, and yet the Department sanctions this inconveniencing of the whole district. Further, the reserve is the resort of the scrag of the district.[11]

John Ridgeway argued strongly against any such moves to have the Aboriginal families pushed from their land. The white pressure group insisted that the Aboriginal families only needed a small piece of the reserve. But in a letter to the Commissioner of Police, Ridgeway stressed that loss of this section — the only watered section of the property — would force the Aboriginal families out. Ridgeway drew attention to the fact that he and his family members had been living on the land for over fifty years, and had first made application for return of the land in 1888. Once granted, in 1891, the families had worked tirelessly to clear and improve the land. They had built homesteads, planted crops and erected fencing. John Ridgeway received strong support from the local police in the area, who responded to white protests with letters of their own:

> Surely after doing all the improvements, for their own benefit, their land is not to be taken from them *because* it is cleared and fenced, to please the whim of any one man. The Reserve is a credit to the Aborigines, and in the senior sergeant's opinion it would be very unfair to remove them and send them into the bush.[12]

Fred Maynard would have been well aware of these fights for land in the early stages of the twentieth century. Older Aboriginal men like William and Johnny Ridgeway helped fan his politically charged fire. Sid Ridgeway, William's son, remained one of Fred Maynard's closest friends, and stood alongside Maynard as an office bearer in the AAPA. (Fred's cousin Cora Robertson eventually married Sid Ridgeway.) The parallel experiences of working on the north coast of New South Wales and witnessing the visible inequality of the Aboriginal experience continued to ferment and

Worimi man, Johnny Ridgeway, was a campaigner for his peoples' rights to land (photo courtesy of Les Ridgeway). His nephew, Sid Ridgeway, was an AAPA office bearer and one of Fred Maynard's closest friends.

percolate in the mind of Fred Maynard during these years. The Maynard children all remember their father's stories of this time, hauling timber from up the coast with an oxen team and his fox terrier — a friend and confidant that he would talk to at night by the light of his campfire.[13]

Mary and David Maynard recall stories told by their father of his days as a prospector and miner, in either the Kimberley or Flinders ranges (opinions differ). Fred Maynard was twenty years old in 1899, already a seasoned drover, horseman and timber-getter, so prospecting was well within his capabilities. The path he took across the range was one used by and well known to drovers. It was a high and narrow path, only wide enough for one horse in some places. Fred lost one of his packhorses over the side, but he went on to have some success in his prospecting career. Despite their childhood poverty his children recalled mementos to show that their father had at some time prospered: a gold tiepin in the shape of Australia with gemstones reflecting the capital cities; a beautiful suit with soft kids shoes, kept from his days as a young man; a top hat which, if you hit it, tipped out. He also had two gold teeth from gold he had found himself.

It would appear that in spite of its distance, Western Australia is the more likely location of Maynard's prospecting days. The Kimberley region exploded with gold fever in 1886. The tracks and paths of the Kimberley were sheer and hard to traverse, and this bears some relevance to the oral story as related to his children. Shortly after the Kimberley rush, gold was discovered at the Pilbara. There is evidence that Aborigines took to prospecting opportunities as a means of improving their lot in life, the same as others from the lower rungs of the economic chain. A miner's rebellion at Bendigo on the Victorian goldfields in the mid-nineteenth century (the 'Red Ribbon' demonstrations) clearly illustrates that Aboriginal people were a part of the goldfields scene. Messner quotes Charles Schmidt, who gave evidence on behalf of German miners during an enquiry into the demonstrations, who noted the presence of Indigenous diggers at Bendigo:

> I saw a native black fellow once taken by the police; and I asked the constable if the black was bound to have a license; and he said he had orders to take every man that had not got a license. There were four or five natives working together, and they made a good bit of gold. They were asked if they had any license, and said no, the country belonged to them, and they were not going to pay a license. They were after all ordered off the diggings. William Howitt also observed Aboriginals amongst the audience of a Bendigo demonstration.[14]

The complex and highly politically attuned make-up of the adult Fred Maynard was the result of many varied and impacting events, experiences and people. The horrific experiences suffered by members of his own family — including his own childhood abandonment and maltreatment as a young boy, and then his subsequent wide travels and observations of the personal suffering and experiences of many other Aboriginal people in differing locations — triggered his own anger. By 1907 Fred Maynard was back in Sydney living in Wooloomooloo with his brother Arthur and working on the Sydney docks as a wharf labourer.

It was here that his bubbling anger took a more political form. The wharf was the place to harden ones resolve and hone a political outlook to a razor edge.

3.

Inspiration and Influences

It is difficult to predict when new pasts will erupt through the surface of established understandings and change the landscape of the future.

David Brion Davis

During the course of the first two decades of the twentieth century Fred Maynard came into contact with an assortment of individuals and environments that influenced, inspired and supported his emerging political directive and ideology. Working on the Sydney docks had a major impact on both his political outlook and his physical and mental strength. The Sydney waterfront was no place for the faint hearted. A wharf labourer named Jack Simpson later recalled the conditions on the docks in Sydney:

> A ghastly, frightening [group] of men at times fighting and tearing each others clothes off in sweating jungle-like scuffles, for a starting docket to earn twenty three shillings for a day's work on the wharves. That was the bull system. Hundreds of men, lines of fear, pain and anguish in their tired faces, walking despondently and dispiritedly up the street.[1]

This horror workplace was known as the 'hungry mile'. The men were savagely exploited 'under the whip of hunger; a hundred tons of lead an hour, 1800 to 2000 bales of wool per gang per eight hours, eighty tons of bagged sugar to be unloaded per hour.[2] There was an almost clan-like mentality on the docks as men from Pyrmont, Sussex Street, Woolloomooloo and Millers Point fought to protect their turf and livelihood from outsiders. The wharf was a hotbed of political fighting with a long history of militancy. The Sydney waterside workers opposed Australia's involvement in the First World War and opposed conscription, taking part in the two conscription referenda and helping to defeat them.

Importantly for Fred Maynard's developing political awareness, the Sydney docks offered contact and communication between Aboriginal men employed as wharf labourers and foreign Black seamen. Understandably, an appreciation of the international Black struggle developed within the mindset of the Aboriginal dockworkers. They realised they were not alone, and others around the globe were speaking out against blatant oppression, racism, and prejudice directed against Black and Indigenous people.

The first indication of serious Black influence upon later Aboriginal political mobilisation is the formation in Sydney in 1903 of an organisation called the Coloured Progressive Association (CPA). The name itself may have had some bearing, seventeen years later, on the name of the Australian Aboriginal Progressive Association. The CPA and its links with Aboriginal people were undoubtedly a result of working connections on the busy Sydney waterfront. The CPA's membership largely comprised of African Americans and West Indians, although evidence reveals that Aboriginal people were also involved.[3] The great majority of the international Black men were foreign seamen. This period in Australia was one that witnessed high levels of overt racism. The White Australia policy was a famous product of the era. International Black commentators were scathing:

> There is Australia, a great empty continent containing five million people where it could easily support one hundred million. It is being held for white settlers who do not come, while coloured people are being kept out. Let Australia open its doors to its natural coloured settlers.[4]

It would have been a forbidding experience for these international Black seamen in Australian ports at the time. One Jamaican seaman displayed his disgust by refusing to turn out for the customs inspection. He was forced to appear in court and replied to the magistrate:

> 'We went to Newcastle, had to pass customs; went to Wallaroo, had to pass customs; came to Port Adelaide had to pass customs. Once I was undressed, and they made me come up. There are 12 of us coloured men on the ship, and we want to know why we should be singled out. The ship is chartered, and we came to work the ship, not to live here. We do not see why we should have to pass the customs every time we come into port.' Defendant was ordered to forfeit two days' pay, and to pay £2 1/- costs. As he left the court he bowed to the magistrate and said, 'Good Morning Sir'.[5]

In 1904 a deck crew of 20 'lascars' (Indian or South-East Asian sailors) had left a ship docked in Melbourne and camped on shore, refusing point blank to return to the vessel. They complained to authorities of ill treatment working on the Australian-owned vessel *Argus* and that they had been assaulted by the captain:

> The 20 Lascar deck hands who struck work on the steamer *Argus* at Williamstown yesterday, walked to Melbourne during the night and this morning they interviewed the shipping master. They explained that their wages ranged from 10 to 35 rupees per month, but that none of it could be handled until they returned to the port from which they shipped.
>
> Eight of the men complained that they had been struck by the captain. They all declined to go on board unless there was a fresh captain. They would sooner go to gaol. After some angry passages, Captain Currie said he would take out warrants and have the men imprisoned till the time of sailing. The charges against the captain were denied by the captain and the first mate.[6]

The following day the men appeared before the city court and received no support to their pleas of abuse. The captain was exonerated and the crewmen brave enough to stand-up in the face of abuse penalised:

> The 21 Lascar seamen who went on strike from the steamer *Argus* on Sunday, owing as they alleged to ill treatment by the captain, were before the city court today. Captain Sutherland said he had not touched any of the men, and he had heard no complaints.
>
> The Bench, after hearing further evidence, ordered 18 of the men back to the steamer, whilst the others, who were said to have caused the trouble, were remanded for a week.[7]

Evidence from twenty years later shows that the conditions for international Black seamen in Australian ports remained harsh. A crew of West African seamen went on strike while their ship was in dock at Newcastle. It was noted in the press that the captain of the vessel would 'have to support them on board or pay a penalty of £100 a man if they remain off the ship more than 24 hours'.[8] Although some white groups opposed the restrictive policies that targeted Black visitors (the Seamen's Union passed a resolution in favour of Black labour on ships in Australian waters[9]) similar severe experiences for Black seamen existed in other ports around the globe during the early decades of the twentieth century. Many Black seamen were forced to live in extreme poverty in English ports such as London, Liverpool, Cardiff and Hull:

> Dumped from tramp steamers or attracted by the prospect of casual work … black seamen found it hard to get another ship, harder still to find work ashore. Most white seamen rejected them as shipmates; white dockers, too, refused to work alongside them. Having spent the small sums they had been paid off with, having pawned any spare clothes

and other belongings, destitute seamen tramped from port to port, desperate for work. Their quest was endless and almost hopeless. Help from compatriots and parish hand-outs kept them from starving.[10]

This connection between Black sailors, Black wharf labourers and communities was not a sudden or recent development. This was a culture of communication, inspiration and connection that had been ongoing around the globe for more than a century. Paul Gilroy's work sought to examine the transatlantic Black movement and connections. This maritime migration of people and ideas was instrumental not only in the passing of goods but also of 'the political struggles that flowed back and forth across the ocean'.[11] Gilroy's work considers 'the global spread of black people which has resulted from a series of forced and voluntary migrations' arguing that this 'binds together the black people of Africa, the Americas, the Caribbean and Europe in a long history of intercultural connection'.[12] The formation of the CPA in Sydney was undoubtedly as a result of similar experiences. Black men and women congregated together for support in the face of mutual hardship and isolation.

***

The CPA itself may never have been noticed and simply faded into oblivion except for the arrival in Australia in 1907 of one extremely high-profile individual. Heavyweight boxer Jack Johnson was one of the most charismatic and talented sporting identities the world had ever known. Certainly the coming of Johnson to Australia gave Aboriginal people an identifiable Black icon of great celebrity to cheer, and to aspire to. Johnson had for years been denied the opportunity of fighting for the world heavyweight championship. He had two fights during his first Australian visit, knocking out both West Indian Peter Felix and Australian Bill Lang. Johnson's ring credentials as an athlete were outstanding. In a career that had thus far spanned some several years he had won an incredible sixty-four out of sixty-five fights, his only loss a highly disputed decision against Marvin Hart in San Francisco the previous year.

Johnson and his manager arrived in Sydney on 24 January 1907. Initial Australian press correspondence was generally complimentary, describing the fighter as 'a fine specimen of manhood' with 'features more regular than those of the average American negro', and the unrecognised 'champion of the world'.[13] Such comments, however, were in the minority. Racial hostility directed at Johnson accelerated over the course of his Australian visit. The *Sydney Sportsman*'s report of Johnson's arrival provides vivid evidence of the racist nature of the media, describing him shamelessly as being 'of the type of the little coons who may be seen devouring watermelons in a well-known American picture'.[14]

The incomparable Jack Johnson, the first black 'Heavyweight Champion of the World' 1907.

Despite his indisputable mastery and skill in the ring, the colour bar had always been drawn heavily against him. 'John L Sullivan, the first modern-era champion, refused to defend against Black contenders and his successors followed the tradition'.[15] At his official reception at the Amphitheatre in Sydney, Mr EH Gardner welcomed Johnson to Australian shores where he was assured 'that in Australia he could rely upon getting a fair deal ... The greatest fighter of them all — Peter Jackson — was coloured but his heart was truly white. They could find nowhere a more gentlemanly or humane man'.[16]

It seems from that statement Johnson had to assume the mantle of a Black–white person.

Johnson certainly had his admirers. One man he had defeated in the ring, Joe Choynski, had gone on to fight and earn great respect in Australia.

Writing from the United States, Choynski said 'Johnson was a white man in the ring, although of color, and one of the best fighters in America. They will not fight him. They bar his color, but it is his cleverness they fear'.[17] They may have wished that he was another Peter Jackson, but there was never a chance of whitewashing Jack Johnson.

Johnson made his first ring appearance in an exhibition against Peter King in Sydney at the Queen's Hall in Pitt Street on 28 January. Johnson was impressive and the *Evening News* stated 'the big coloured man upheld his reputation for cleverness … and the opinion of the "sports" present was that he will be about the hottest thing in the ring business that has been seen here for years'.[18]

Johnson's full-fight debut in Australia was made at the Gaiety Athletic Hall in Sydney, on 28 February 1907. This fight, against the West Indian Peter Felix, had been tagged in the media as the 'Coloured Heavyweight' title fight and had been eagerly awaited. A large crowd packed into the club. The fight itself was no contest as Johnson won in a canter; it was all over in two minutes and twenty seconds. Johnson's next appearance, against Bill Lang at Richmond Racecourse in Melbourne, saw the highest purse offered in an Australian boxing match to that time. Despite torrential rain a crowd of between 15,000 and 20,000 people turned out,[19] but again the fight was one-sided. Johnson (just as Muhammad Ali would six decades later) refused the stool between rounds and stood in his corner soaking up both the rain and the constant racial abuse of the crowd.[20] The fight ended when Johnson knocked out Lang in the ninth round.

An advertisement in the *Referee* on 13 March 1907 drew attention to Johnson's imminent return to the United States, and that an organising body called the Coloured Progressive Association of New South Wales was holding a farewell function in his honour. The organisation was described as a 'solid influential Sydney body'.[21]

The farewell, held at Leigh House in Sydney, was evidently well attended and an undoubted success, but was given sarcastic racist coverage by the *Truth*, which reported 'the gorgeous mirrors of the dance-room reflected the gyrations of the coloured cult of the city…white men (a very few) ambled around with full black, half and quarter caste beauties'.[22]

Jack Johnson was depicted as looking magnificent when he arrived in a light, square-cut tweed suit. He moved at ease among the crowd throughout the evening but did not take to the dance floor himself. Highlights of the dancing during the night presents further evidence of the maritime background of those present 'a quadrille was in progress shortly after 11 o'clock, and some sable dancers were displaying bell bottomed trousers with great effect'.[23]

The Coloured Progressive Association of New South Wales in 1907, at a dinner to farewell Jack Johnson (at the back in light tweed) after his winning fight.

Despite its glaringly offensive tone, the article represents historical evidence of the CPA at the time. The president, an elderly 'coloured' gentleman and a former steam-tug captain, W Grant, indicated to the reporter that the organisation had established a membership of '40 or 50 and had been in existence about four years'.[24]

> He also let it be distinctly understood that the Black Progressives didn't like the Commonwealth restrictive legislation. They want an Open Black Door, which coons can enter at their own sweet will.[25]

The journalist completely dismissed the thought that Aboriginal people could have been a part of the evening. Obviously educated and elegantly attired Aboriginal men and women were out of the realm of his imagination:

> Comfortably disposed about the lounges were ladies white and coloured. Some of the latter were full-blown [N]egresses, and there was a mixture of half-castes, quadroons and octoroons. On each side of the ballroom were seated black wallflowers, interspersed with a few whites. The coloured gentlemen and ladies were almost entirely of the American type. The Coloured Progress Association does not evidently include the La Perouse shade.[26]

But a photograph of the event shows that Fred Maynard was present at Johnson's farewell.[27] This photograph has been wrongly attributed in the past as being an AAPA meeting in Sydney during the 1920s — yet it clearly identifies Jack Johnson and the West Indian boxer Peter Felix.[28] No further mention or account of the CPA has to date been found.

Johnson was at home among Black seamen and dock workers. As a young man he was employed as a dock worker in Galveston, Texas. In fact, it was on the docks that he began his climb to boxing immortality.

Johnson had displayed interest, knowledge and appreciation of traditional Aboriginal life during his visit. 'I spend most of my spare time in the art galleries and the museum,' he stated.

> My principle hobby is archaeology. When I visit your museum and see the numerous specimens of prehistoric man's art, your boomerangs of many varieties, your stone axes from various States and the many examples of Paleolithic and Neolithic man's skill — simply I envy you. America had its rude implements but they did not show anything like the same foresight. The Australian natives must have been geniuses to invent such weapons.[29]

Johnson was afraid of no-one and insisted on being treated with respect. This was completely beyond the understanding of the majority of white people who expected and demanded that blacks knew their place. On 18 March, the day after Johnson's farewell, Johnson broke the nose of his white manager AA McLean, and was charged with assault at the Water Police Court in Sydney. The *Sydney Sportsman* reported that 'McLean called Johnson a big black b-----, whereupon the nigger knocked him down'; Johnson was fined £5 and £1 1s costs in default of a two months' prison sentence, which he paid and then departed.[30] It was this sort of behaviour that signalled to Black people across the globe, including Australia, that they did not have to be subservient to any one.

In his final interview Johnson may have been having a little tongue-in-cheek dig at the locals:

> I wish to thank all Australians through you for the splendid manner in which they have treated me during the whole of my stay in their country. I wish to thank them one and all from the bottom of my heart. I could not have been treated better even in my own country. I may say from what I have seen of your country it is a grand one, and the people — well, all I can say of them is that they are a fine broad-minded lot of fellows. The only fault I have to find with them is that they are too liberal. Had I been inclined I could have had one continual round of amusement — dinners, banquets and other things.

That is their only fault and had I not been very careful — well, I don't know what would have happened. [31]

Late in 1908 Johnson returned to Australia to fight the Canadian world champion Tommy Burns for the heavyweight championship. It is worth noting that Johnson was given the privilege of official exemption to enter the country to take part in the fight.[32] Burns was offered the incredible sum of £6000 to defend his title; against Johnson in Sydney. Johnson was to receive £1000 for the fight and under the circumstances of being denied the opportunity for so long he would probably have climbed into the ring for nothing.[33]

Next to the Melbourne 1956 Olympic Games, this fight remains as the biggest sporting event with an international focus staged in Australia during the twentieth century. It was held at the specially constructed open-air Sydney Stadium. It was a sell out, with 20,000 people jammed into the stadium and a further 40,000 locked outside. Johnson completely destroyed Burns, and all the years of racial prejudice, persecution and denied opportunity spurred him on. During the fight Johnson taunted Burns that he punched like a woman, that Mrs Burns would not recognise him when he got home. Burns was knocked down three times in the first two rounds, but Johnson had no intention of ending it early. He was like a cat playing with a mouse. The beating Burns took was so complete that the police eventually jumped into the ring and stopped the punishment.

The news of this great Black victory spread around the globe and rapidly through the Aboriginal and Islander communities where it was received with jubilation. A Solomon Islander who was present at the Burns–Johnson fight as a young boy later described it as 'the greatest day of my life'.[34] Years later Johnson himself recounted that during the break between rounds, his eyes surveyed the crowd, and he drew strength from a Black man he saw in the audience:

> As my gaze wandered out into the surrounding territory, I saw a colored man sitting on a fence watching the fight with open mouth and bulging eyes. My glance returned to him again and again. He was one of the very few colored people present, and he became a sort of landmark for me. [35]

Fears of the consequences of such identification of Black Australians with Johnson's victory underlay attempts to suppress the news of Johnson's win in such places as the Solomon Islands, where it was felt 'the "natives" might take an inappropriate message from it'.[36] A writer in the *Bulletin* screamed 'Johnson's behavior in the ring was objectionable…if it had happened in America, someone would have shot him dead to the cheers of the crowd and given the film as defense evidence and got a verdict of "justifiable homicide".'[37] Randolph Bedford, writing for the Melbourne *Herald*, did not hold back in his scorn of Johnson. 'Already the insolent black's victory causes skin troubles in Woolloomooloo,' he moaned. 'An hour after, I heard a lascar laying down the law of Queensberry to two whites, and they listened humbly. It is a bad day for Australia'.[38] Bedford's article incited a debate that raged on the letters page of the Melbourne *Herald*. However one writer, simply signed as 'Uncle Tom', commented dryly:

> Reverse the conditions which prevailed at Sydney and place a white boxer in a ring in a southern State in America, with a huge crowd of hostile blacks, it would be pardonable if he replied to their taunts as Johnson did on Saturday. If Jack Johnson's critics are not satisfied with him I might remind them that there are millions of highly cultured colored gentlemen in America and other parts of the world who possess as high an order of intelligence, and certainly more humanity, than Mr. Randolph Bedford.[39]

The significance and impact that Jack Johnson made on the international Black population around the globe cannot be underestimated. Johnson returned to the United States where he knocked out Stanley Ketchel, and then the 'Great White Hope', Jim Jeffries. After the Johnson–Jeffries fight, race riots erupted in the United States. Whites reacted angrily when Johnson seemed to toy with Jeffries before knocking him out in the fifteenth round. The violence of the ensuing riots made worldwide headlines.[40] The whole assumption and unquestioned aura of white supremacy had been firmly knocked out by Jack Johnson.

The joy that Aboriginal people had taken in Johnson's victory over Burns in Sydney had not abated, and evidence reveals that they continued to follow his exploits around the globe.

A squatter on the north coast of NSW, Cunningham Henderson, later recorded his memories of the Johnson–Jeffries fight. Henderson's recollections offer a valuable insight of the differing Black and white sentiments surrounding this major sporting event. Henderson recalled that he was helping his friend, Tom Yabsley, to muster cattle:

> It was the day of the Johnson–Jeffries fight in America. Because of Johnson's colour the black boys took a keen interest in the fight and were discussing it. Just then a blasting shot went off in a stone quarry a few miles away, which we heard plainly. Yabsley turned quickly to Alfie and said 'Did you hear that?' 'Yes, Boss. What that feller?' 'That was Jeffries hitting Johnson!' Alfie quickly cupped his hand, held it to his ear, and striking a listening attitude, said 'No, Boss, I never heard the people shout!' (meaning there was no applause). The laugh was against the boss.[41]

The fact that Henderson remembered this incident, that he recalled the Aboriginal men discussing the fight and the superficially light-hearted banter between the whites and blacks about it, all suggest that its significance ran deeply for them all.

Jack Johnson went on to hold the world title for another seven years, but eventually fled the United States because of trumped up charges of trafficking white women. In 1915 Johnson lost the title in Havana to Jess Willard, although controversy over the decision and aftermath of the fight rage to this day. (Johnson claimed that he was made an offer that if he lost the fight the charges against him would be dropped and he could return to the States. He did return but was jailed for nine months, and though he returned to boxing was never given the chance to regain the lost title.) Along with Joe Louis, Sugar Ray Robinson and Muhammad Ali, Johnson is regarded as one of the greatest fighters of all time, and an inspiration to future generations of Black athletes. The dominance that white society had held and obviously believed was seriously shaken through his triumphs. In this context he was a trailblazer of Black inspiration, self-belief and triumph.

Many of the deeply embedded stereotypes of supposed white physical and mental superiority — the social Darwinism of the late-nineteenth century — were swept away by Johnson. The impact was not just confined to his own era, but continued to confound and confuse theorists for decades.

Marcus Garvey, who himself would figure prominently as a rallying and inspirational figure for Aboriginal Australians, once declared 'a strong man is strong everywhere'[42] and Jack Johnson was such a man. He was, Garvey said, 'strong everywhere he went. He had beaten his white opponent in Australia, he had beaten them in the United States and he could beat them wherever they presented themselves. He was strong, and it did not matter where you took him, he was still strong'.[43]

There is little doubt that Aboriginal wharf labourers continued their association with international Black seamen prior to, during and after the First World War. From 1903 to 1935, 335 international Black people entered and left Australian ports, and the six-year period between 1912 and 1917 saw 106 of these international Black visitors enter and leave Sydney.[44] The acceleration of contact between Aboriginal wharf laborers in Sydney and visiting Black seamen during this period of world turmoil could well have set the foundation for the launch of Aboriginal political agitation in 1924.

The First World War was a catalyst for great change, as was its conclusion. The western imperial powers had been weakened and their position of expansionist superiority seriously eroded. The war strongly affected Black protestors in the United States and Africa, with one Black speaker at a New York branch of the Universal Negro Improvement Association (UNIA) meeting in 1922 passionately declaring:

> You are asked to go and fight the Germans who had done you no wrong. You were told to give the Germans hell, while they were giving you hell over here, and while you were giving the Germans hell, they were giving your mothers, sisters and sons hell in Mississippi, Georgia, Alabama and then the Negro asked 'Which is better, to make the world safe for democracy, or to make his home safe for his wife and children?' That is what he asked then and what he is asking now.[45]

Around the world many oppressed groups, including Indigenous peoples, gained in confidence and found a political voice. Many of these groups were inspired and fuelled with a driving surge of national and cultural pride and their political agenda was driven under the banner of 'self-determination'. The concepts of self-reliance and self-determination are associated with various forms of Black Nationalism, most notably with Gandhi and Marcus Garvey.

This upsurge in protest internationally was reflected in Australia with the rise of the Australian Aboriginal Progressive Association, which drew its inspiration from and would mirror many of the demands of these international Black groups. A significant factor of the period globally was the move from rural environments to the cities of many Black people seeking better working opportunities. This was reflected in the nucleus of the 1920s Aboriginal political movement; men like Fred Maynard, Tom Lacey, Dick Johnson and Sid Ridgeway were all working and living in Sydney and not confined to reserves.

The international Black political surge reflected a strong push for equal political, economic and social rights. But significantly for the rise of Aboriginal political protest, 'focusing on them to the exclusion of cultural issues could not satisfy the need of a people who had been humiliated by white supremacy for sources of group pride and a positive sense of identity'.[46] Through their contacts with African American seamen on the docks and waterfront of Sydney the Aboriginal leaders of the 1920s acquired knowledge of the works of Frederick Douglas, Booker T Washington, WEB Du Bois and Marcus Garvey. It is therefore understandable that international Black movements and ideologies would form the core of the political directives and rhetoric of the Aboriginal leaders.

A number of sources illustrate that these international Black writers and many more were available and sought in Australia. A letter sent to Carter G Woodson, editor of the *Journal of Negro History* (and regarded by many as the 'Father of Negro History'), proves that point. The letter once more hints to the maritime connection, as writer, A Goldsmith (self-described as a 'Negro Exile') sent his correspondence to Woodson from Port Melbourne in 1920. Goldsmith informed Woodson that the 'Negro papers I read out here [are] *The Crisis*, the *Brownies Book, Crusader, Journal of Negro History*, the *Negro World*, the *Emancipator*'.[47] Goldsmith inquired of Woodson's intellectual appraisal: 'What do you think of them?' He enclosed 9/- 6d to Woodson for his subscription for the *Negro History* journal.

Future AAPA leader Tom Lacey's letter to Amy Jaques Garvey in 1924 substantiates the Australian interest in international Black literature and newspapers. Lacey hinted at their propaganda potential. 'I would be very grateful to you if you could advise me how to get some of your American papers, the *Negro World* and other papers, so that I could distribute them among our people as it might help to enlighten them a bit'.[48]

It is important to consider not just the impact of newspapers like the *Negro World* but the attempts by white authorities to stamp out their circulation. 'The *Negro World* penetrated every area where Black folk lived and had regular readers as far away as Australia':

> It was cited by colonial powers as a factor in uprisings and unrest in such diverse places as Dahomey, British Honduras, Kenya, Trinidad and Cuba. These powers therefore had no illusions concerning the appeal of its message of racial self-reliance and its anticolonialist tone to oppressed black people. During its entire existence, therefore, the paper was engaged in a running battle with the British, French, United States and other governments, all of which assiduously sought to engineer its demise, or, failing that, to restrict or prevent its circulation.[49]

Many later notables — including Elijah Muhammed, Malcolm X, Martin Luther King and Ho Chi Minh — acknowledged the influence of Garveyism. King stated that Garvey 'was the first man of colour in the history of the United States to lead and develop a mass movement. He was the first man on a mass scale and level to give millions of Negroes a sense of dignity and destiny and make the Negroe feel he was somebody'.[50] Malcolm X drew similar conclusions: 'All the freedom movements that are taking place right here in America today were initiated by the work and teachings of Marcus Garvey'.[51] Vietnamese leader Ho Chi Minh is recognised as the Third World leader who had the closest connection to the UNIA'. As a young man Ho had been a seaman 'and he once spent a few months in New York. The Garvey movement interested him greatly and he regularly attended UNIA meetings'.[52]

The rapid rise of Marcus Garvey had begun soon after his arrival in the United States from Jamaica in 1916, and inside one year he had established the UNIA in New York. In the early stages the organisation relied upon Black Jamaicans for its membership and support base. But greater racial consciousness in the aftermath of First World War was instrumental in attracting thousands of African American supporters especially in Harlem.

> In January 1918, he launched the *Negro World*, a newspaper that Claude McKay, another Jamaican dubbed 'the best-edited coloured weekly in New York'. In 1919 an attack on his life led to further publicity for Garvey as a persecuted martyr.[53]

Garvey's organisation experienced phenomenal growth and spread across the globe with unbelievable speed. The UNIA stirred 'the entire world of Negroes to a consciousness of race pride, which never existed before' and broke down 'the barriers of racial nationality among Negroes and caused American, African, West Indian, Canadian, Australian and South and Central American Negroes to realise they have a common interest'.[54] Garvey insisted the UNIA did not exclude anyone:

> For once we will agree with the American white man, that one drop of Negro blood makes a man a Negro. In the UNIA 100 per cent Negroes and even 1 per cent Negroes will stand together as one mighty whole.[55]

Once again, the world's wharfs prove to be a pivotal connection, with Garvey able to achieve a worldwide network of information by sending out agents to spread his message, and many 'of those who did this work for him were seamen'.[56] A Federal Bureau of Investigation report on Garvey and his activities in 1919 revealed the unease over his far-reaching message. 'Garvey's office on 135th Str. is sort of a clearing house for all international radical agitators, including Mexicans, South Americans, Spaniards, in fact black and yellow from all parts of the globe who radiate around Garvey'.[57]

At the height of its power in the mid 1920s the UNIA had successfully established chapters in 41 countries, including branch number 646 in Australia:

> The Sydney, Australia UNIA branch was undoubtedly the furthest from Harlem. It illustrated how, in those days before even the widespread use of radio, Garvey and the UNIA were nevertheless able to draw communities from practically all over the world together into a single organization with a single aim.[58]

In August 1920, the UNIA held the first of a number of highly successful international conventions, and over 25,000 members gathered at Madison Square Garden in New York to hear Garvey speak. UNIA branch members from as far away as Australia, Africa and North America attended.[59]

The identities of the Australian delegates present at that convention remains a mystery. However, the *Negro World* reveals some information of the background and activities of the Sydney UNIA branch. A letter sent by the secretary, Robert Usher, and published in 1923 indicates the excitement and enthusiasm of the Sydney group, and that the impact of Garvey and his organisation was 'resounding throughout the length and breadth of this small continent'.[60]

Despite some difficulties the branch was up and running and money was being spent to ensure its growth. Usher revealed that many Black people in Australia were suffering low self-esteem and confidence 'but there are some of us who are doing our best to not only keep ourselves out of the mire, but to pull our brothers out as well'.[61] The Sydney branch was adamant that it intended to push information of Garveyism to break ignorance within Aboriginal communities and provide inspiration: 'we are doing our best to bring them in line'.[62] Usher was aware of Garvey's proposed world tour and expressed the hope he might include an Australian visit.[63] A United States federal surveillance report reveals that in 1923 Garvey had taken steps to undertake a world tour, including a month in Australia.[64] Garvey himself had no hesitation in recognising the support and loyalty of the Sydney branch:

> The moment I landed in New York I received a cable from Sydney, Australia, where we have a division, who manifested their loyalty 100 per cent, after hearing and reading in the Sydney papers of my arrest here a few weeks ago.[65]

The letter from future AAPA treasurer Tom Lacey to Amy Jaques Garvey, written in 1924, helps clarify the makeup and operation of the Sydney branch. It delivers conclusive evidence of Aboriginal involvement with the Sydney UNIA branch. Lacey's letter pledged the support of 10,000 Aboriginal people in NSW and 60,000 Aboriginal people nationally to Garvey and his movement.[66] Lacey revealed that the Sydney UNIA was looking to expand and had a national focus at the forefront of its agenda. 'We have not had the time to organize the other four states yet, but I think there are about fifty or sixty thousand; that is as far as we can reach at the present time'.[67] Lacey pointed out that he himself had been a member of the Sydney UNIA branch for four years (that is, since 1920) and had recently been elected as the organisor of the Sydney chapter.

His letter clearly reveals that the Aboriginal political fight was hampered by the tight control exerted over many Aboriginal people confined on reserves by both missionaries and government Aboriginal Protection Boards.

> I hope before long you will be able to send us a delegate down here to Australia, as it would mean a great help to us...We have a bit of trouble to see some of our people, as the missionaries have got the most of them, and we have great difficulty in reaching them. The authorities won't allow us to see them unless we can give them (the Aboriginal Board) a clear explanation of what we want them for.[68]

He recognised the negative long-term affect of confinement on missions and reserves for the Aboriginal population. The authorities 'have got their minds so much doped that they think they can never become a people'.[69]

Lacey revealed that his sister was also involved with the Sydney UNIA branch and offered some evidence that Aboriginal people in Australia had taken up the initiative to inform the international Black community of their plight in Australia.

During the 1920s the *Negro World* provided a well-informed coverage of the Aboriginal situation in Australia to its international Black readership. Numerous articles appeared, for example, highlighting the rise of a white humanitarian movement to establish a 'Model Aboriginal Black State' in northern Australia,[70] commentary on the restrictive White Australia policy, and the use of violence directed against the Aboriginal population.[71] Headline banners delivered vivid imagery of the Australian Aboriginal experience — 'Race Horrors in Australia Unspeakably Vile'[72] and 'Killing off the Black Australians'.[73] The latter article explained to its readers that a great number of Aboriginal people were caged on government reserves 'and were being rapidly aided by so-called civilised man to join the extinct types'.[74] A comparison with the experience of Indigenous Americans was drawn:

> It is hardly believable that the white rulers of Australia, who have taken the country by force from the blacks, as they took the North American continent from the Red Men, have dealt with the black natives in a spirit of exterminating them root and branch, and with no regard whatsoever for the humanities.[75]

A report summarising the influence and impact of Garveyism around the globe in 1924, was titled 'Blacks of Australia enslaved and brutalised':

> Everywhere the black man is beginning to do his own thinking, to demand more participation in his own government, more economic justice, and better living conditions. The Universal Negro Improvement

Association during the past five years has blazed the trail for him, and he is following the trail. We do not think he will turn back. He has nothing to lose and everything to gain by pushing forward, whatever the obstacles he may encounter.[76]

During these years there was widespread media condemnation and fear of Garvey and his movement in the mainstream white Australian press. Many of the articles were both racist and alarmist in their content.

> Little is known in Europe of the movement of revolt and protest, which the New York International Congress of the negro-peoples of the world represents, but it is not to be ignored. It is a part of the menace to the domination of the white races, and it is vitally connected with the ever increasing power of Japan and the movement among the Moslems. The New York Congress began with a procession of negroes, many of them in elaborate uniforms, and among the banners was one depicting a black Virgin Mary leaning over a black child. This banner was a crude summary of the movement. The white man's domination is no longer accepted as inevitable, his predominance is frankly challenged.[77]

One paranoid writer in the *Nambucca and Bellinger News* in 1925 highlighted the levels of racist hysteria present at the time. The writer warned that the white race was in decline and decay 'not in culture or intellect, but numerically; the black race is growing swiftly, relentlessly, ruthlessly for all the rest of us, but for the whites especially. In 100 years from now the blacks may be supreme'.[78]

The article was an undoubted attempt to inflame the passions of the ignorant. The UNIA had established all-Black factories and an all-Black steamship line but was forced into collapse through the actions of the authorities. The writer saw this as in all likelihood only a temporary setback:

> The hard fact remains, however, that in a relatively short campaign the League had from a nucleus of some fifteen stalwarts to a membership of somewhere in the neighbourhood of 2,000,000 organised in hundreds of branches; that it won a good deal of plausible sympathy; that many short-sighted Americans even saw in the negro prophet's dream of a 'Back to Africa' campaign a possible solution of the immediate problems in their own continent; and that there are some 400,000,000 negros in the world population in the world already with a power of prolific expansion shown by no other race.[79]

Another report in the *Adelaide Advertiser* confirmed the fears and ignorance portrayed to the wider community of Marcus Garvey and his organisation. Garvey was described as a man who:

looks to the time when the yellow and white races will be locked in a great race war, the negroe's [sic] will march over their weakened and prostrate bodies and enter into their own. The bloodiest of all wars is yet to come when Europe will match its strength against Asia and that will be the negroe's opportunity to draw the sword for Africa.[80]

However, Garvey and his Universal Negro Improvement Association went into rapid decline between 1923 and 1924. The decline is largely attributed to internal factionalism and persecution by agents of the United States government.[81] Garvey was gaoled in 1923 and was not released until 1927. Shortly after, he was deported from the United States and was denied the opportunity ever to return. Without his inspiring and charismatic leadership, the organisation quickly fell into decline. By the mid 1930s — in the space of only one decade — the organisation and Garveyism itself had all but been erased from memory in the United States. Despite the total collapse and disappearance of the UNIA in such rapid fashion, it remains 'the largest organised mass-based movement of Black People — and by far the most internationalist one — to ever be established in the US. Moreover, its influence is still felt in a number of areas'.[82]

As I shall go on to show, one can only draw similar parallels with the experience of the Australian Aboriginal Progressive Association in Australia. The early Aboriginal political agenda was very much influenced by contact with international Black men and women, and their literature. The AAPA would formulate its political platform from decades of experience and knowledge of international Black issues.

4.
Political Mobilisation

This beautiful world History, is, in Heraclitiean terms, 'a chaotic pile of rubbish'. What is strong wins: that is the universal law. If only it were not so often precisely what is stupid and evil.

Friedrich Nietzsche

As the twentieth century unfolded in the new Australia, Aboriginal people continued to suffer in the wake of dispossession; we continued to be stripped of our land, resources, culture and children. The year 1901 witnessed the federation of the Australian colonies and the creation of a national state across the entire continent: the Commonwealth of Australia.

From an Aboriginal perspective, however, there was little joy or celebration in the federation celebrations of 1901. Aboriginal people were driven to the very margins of existence in an even more organised and articulated fashion — an existence that was at the time thought by most to encompass only a short term. We were considered and widely described as a vanishing race, a relic of the Stone Age. We were denied the right to vote in Commonwealth elections, were not counted in the census, and issues concerning Aboriginal people continued to be under the stringent, regimented control of state rather than Commonwealth legislation. As a result we were not even considered as Australians and were made to suffer and bear the full impact of that ignorance. The myths made by the popular media about a dying race were widely accepted by ordinary Australians

By 1920, Aboriginal people in New South Wales were experiencing horrifying levels of revocation of their hard-worked-for farms and were suffering under the full weight and repercussions of the systematic and sudden removal of their children from their families. The 1915 amendment to the New South Wales *Aboriginal Protection Act* of 1909 gave the Board and its array of bureaucrats the powers and provisions to remove any Aboriginal child from its parent for, in practice, little or no reason other than the fact that they were Aboriginal. The amendment as a published statement gives a very clear indication of the Board's intentions and basis for practice, especially about the perceived future of Aboriginal people.

The initial Act of 1909 had not quite delivered the Board the far-reaching and absolute control it desired. Documented archival evidence abounds of the intentions of the Board prior to 1915. In 1909 the Board argued the need for the 'power to assume full control and custody of the child of any Aborigine if such course shall be deemed by the Board to be in the full interest of such child, and the Board may thereupon remove such child to such control as the Board may care and decide upon'.[1] In 1911, with the presentation of its annual report, the Board dictated that the 'only chance these children have is to be taken away from their present environment and properly trained … before being apprenticed out, and once having left the Aborigines reserves they should never be allowed to return to them permanently'.[2] Both the Board's actions and words were explicit and direct. There was to be no compromise: 'the whole object of the Board was to put things into train on lines that would eventually lead to the camps being depleted of their population, and finally the closing of the reserves and camps altogether'.[3] They stated emphatically that 'it has been the policy of the Board not to allow children, many of whom are almost white, who have been removed from camp life to return thereto, but to eventually merge themselves in the white population'.[4] The practice and directive was premeditated racial and cultural genocide. Aboriginal children were to be taken away and over time swallowed up without trace into the wider white Australian society.

The 1915 amendment did not pass through parliament without some debate and controversy. Colonial Secretary JH Cann stated that the main principle behind the amendment was 'to empower the Board to take the place of the parents'.[5] Mr P McGarry, the sitting member for Murrumbidgee, questioned, does this not 'mean to steal the child away from its parents?' Cann replied that it is 'not a question of stealing the children, but of saving them … from immoral Aboriginal women'.[6] The debate intensified into a heated exchange, and McGarry was forthright in his claim that Aboriginal parents loved their children just as much as anyone else. He went on to articulate the full impact of colonisation: 'We have overrun their country and taken away their domain. We now propose further acts of cruelty upon them by separating the children from the parents'.[7] But the clear-thinking McGarry was a voice crying in a wilderness of prejudice and racial superiority.

In a 1915 meeting of the New South Wales Legislative Council members discussed the intended amendment. One speaker (a MP who was, in fact, also a Board member) rose and spoke against the intended Bill:

> At Darlington Point I have heard an aborigine, who was highly educated, explaining in the best of English how the aborigines were being plundered of their rations, robbed of their lands, and reduced to the position of slaves ... when you meet men who understand all these things, you cannot expect them to calmly submit to an order to take from them their girl or boy in order to place them in a Government institution.[8]

By 1920, Fred Maynard had built up his full repertoire of oratory and written skills and had enhanced and continued to hone his deep political

Fred Maynard and his sister Emma at the Rocks in Sydney, 1927.

knowledge of national and international events and key issues of minority peoples. His experience and knowledge of the deeply felt loss of his Uncle Tom Phillips's land at St Clair near Singleton, and the similar experiences suffered by the Ridgeways on the lower and mid-north coast of New South Wales, had hardened his resolve. These experiences were reinforced by Maynard's years on the wharf, his experiences with the trade union movement and his contact with African Americans. The fervour of the moment was further intensified by the experiences of the First World War in which hundreds of thousands had lost their lives and the world was changed forever.

Aboriginal men had enlisted and travelled overseas to fight for their country. Many of these men lost their lives and those who returned to Australia carried the scars and memories of their horrifying experiences on the battlefronts at Gallipoli, Belgium and France. When they returned home the impact of the perceived insignificance of their sacrifices by the wider white community was slammed home. While they had been away fighting in dreadful conditions some of these men's children had been removed from their wives by the Aboriginal Protection Board.[9] Unlike their white comrades at arms they were not afforded full recognition or community status when they returned. The Aboriginal returned servicemen reverted to being treated as blacks with no rights. When the Soldier Settlement Scheme was introduced by the government to assist the returning heroes in acquiring property, the Aboriginal soldiers found it did not apply to them and not to bother applying.[10]

Dick Johnson was one of those soldiers. He and Fred Maynard became lifelong friends. Johnson, still with vivid memories of the war front, undertook another call-to-arms as he rose to stand alongside Maynard in his fight for Aboriginal political rights and social justice. These Aboriginal leaders' awareness and commitment to their task was unwavering, and with good reason. The 1920 Aborigines Protection Board *Annual Report* draws reference to its intention to eliminate the lighter-caste people from reserves and missions. The 1921 report was even more horrifying and graphic in its language and intention: 'the process of eliminating quadroons and octoroons is being quietly carried out!'[11] it claimed with absolute confidence.

***

The AAPA and its leaders drew influence and inspiration from inter-national Black connections, but this does not devalue the fact that they had a number of white sympathisers and campaigners who stepped into this cauldron of discontent to lend support — most notably Elizabeth McKenzie Hatton and John J Moloney. These two individuals could clearly see and identify the inequality forced upon Aboriginal people and they rallied to assist in opposing the powers that be in the world of government.

From the earliest point of settlement onwards, many individuals came forward with ideas about what the non-Indigenous authorities could best do to 'help' Aboriginal people. The majority of these were put forward with no consultation with or input from Aboriginal people. The major thrust of assistance was in terms of christianising, civilising, caring for or saving a 'doomed race'. At this time the British Empire was one 'on which the sun never sets', and it was considered by the British themselves that they had attained the highest point of human progress and development. Wealthy socialites, working class heroes, righteous intellectuals, or those imbued with nationalistic fervour stepped forth to aid Aboriginal people, especially in the early decades of the twentieth century. Many were white women simply in need of an interest, or campaigning for the feminist platform. Despite many of these people having good intentions, deeply ingrained assumptions and perceptions of European superiority undermined much of their work. These ingrained assumptions were the unchallenged staple of the day, and one woman who initially carried much of the baggage of the period was Elizabeth McKenzie Hatton. However, unlike others, Hatton — through her contact with Aboriginal people — was to undergo a major shift in thinking that was decades ahead of its time. Her alliance with the AAPA in New South Wales resulted in her total opposition to the church, state and her own Christian beliefs.

Elizabeth McKenzie Hatton, affectionately known [by Aboriginal people] as 'Mrs Mac', was a white missionary and well-known social worker. She experienced several family tragedies during her life. She lost her first husband, missionary Jim McKenzie, to a shark attack at Bundaberg.[12] He had conducted a service one hot Sunday, and was returning across the dunes with 'a young Kanaka', when he decided to cool off in the surf. 'The young lad tried to talk him out of swimming on the Lord's Day, but he dived in and was almost immediately taken by a shark. The young boy was so upset he refused to leave the spot for 10 days'.[13]

In 1908 she married again, to Tom Hatton, considered 'to be a bit of a rebel and was very active in various groups'. Hatton was 'a Protestant Irishman and very vocal', and fought for the rights of everyday people — the worker'.[14] (There is some suggestion that Tom Hatton may have been responsible for the couple falling out with their employers at the mission, the cane-growing Young family. He 'was a reformer opposed against social inequality' and he took issue with the harsh conditions under which many of the Islanders were subjected working in the local cane industry.[15])

However, six days prior to her marriage to Hatton, tragedy struck again when Elizabeth's eleven-year old daughter Hope died.

In the aftermath of her first husband's death Elizabeth spent some years with the Islander community at Pialba–Hervey Bay.[16] An Aboriginal missionary, Mrs Charles Aurora, worked closely with Hatton during those years. McKenzie Hatton described Aurora as a 'woman carrying a high standard of Christian character — a clever, refined, and educated woman, she has been used to help in the translation of the scriptures in the language of the Solomon Islands.'[17] During this period she was in touch with Aboriginal people living within the region and about forty Aboriginal people at Tweed Heads 'had heard the gospel mainly through intermarriage with the Kanakas and McKenzie Hatton's work amongst the latter'.[18]

McKenzie Hatton had hoped to go to the Torres Strait originally. Writing to Retta Dixon Long, the AIM missionary, in 1910 she said:

> I am deeply disappointed at not being able to go … I would very much like to join your Mission but I am hindered at present … I have our father to keep now. He is getting on in years & has occasional attacks of asthma.[19]

Further family tragedy, and government indifference, affected McKenzie Hatton's outlook in the coming years. During the First World War she took up pen and paper to assist the war effort, as Hatton's son Stewart from her first marriage to Jim McKenzie had enlisted and was wounded in France. He was flown to a hospital in England and then brought home to Australia as a quadriplegic. He died shortly after his return through infection from his wounds.[20]

The Hatton's were operating a small toy manufacturing company in Melbourne at the time, and McKenzie Hatton requested assistance from the government for expenses incurred in the hospital treatment of her son. She had argued that 'her son was paralysed and as he was not given good attention and was not happy in the military hospital, she took him away to a private hospital and treatment incurring expenses up to about £50'. Not for the first or last time in her life McKenzie Hatton's appeal to government officialdom was to be met with a firm rebuttal and with no empathy for her loss:

> This woman would have had to sign a certificate freeing the Defence Dept from all responsibility in connection with her son if she took him away from hospital.[21]

During these years McKenzie Hatton published several books and booklets on her experiences with South Sea Islanders and life as a missionary in

Queensland. She also wrote a pamphlet, *On Eagle's Wings*, which was a message to other grieving mothers and wives who had lost loved ones during the war. In the foreword one Edward Isaac wrote that he 'knew of nothing more calculated to help the stricken parents of our brave fallen soldier lads'. The insight and understanding expressed by McKenzie Hatton came from one whose 'sensitive spirit had been wounded to the quick'. The pamphlet delivers, in McKenzie Hatton's graphic words, the shock that befalls a mother with the loss of a child:

> Into our home came the sad message one day, 'Your son seriously wounded in France'. O the choking agony of that moment, 'seriously wounded'! O the stab of those words! What would the next message be? And swiftly the mind ran forward with anxious fear. How do we mothers live through such moments? With lightning flash our minds go back to that day, long ago, when the little baby was first clasped in our arms; that day of sweetest memory when with glad and grateful wonder, we called him all our own; and now he is 'seriously wounded' somewhere in France.[22]

The experiences of constant wartime correspondence were to come to the fore a decade letter with her prolific letter writing and petitioning on behalf of the AAPA and the Aboriginal political fight. Her efforts during the war were recognised by the Rev. W Cleugh Black who 'spoke in eulogistic terms of Mrs Hatton's splendid work with her pen during the war, when by such means she brought comfort to thousands of stricken hearts'.[23] In stark contrast to her efforts on behalf of Great War soldiers, however, her later alignment and stance alongside Aboriginal political campaigners a decade later was to meet with ridicule, opposition and open hostility.

After the war, McKenzie Hatton continued her efforts for returned soldiers and grieving families as 'the organising secretary of the Soldiers Mothers Band and is also superintendent of the Missionary Hostel at St James Park, Hawthorne'.[24] This work was interrupted when, after fourteen years' service in the Solomon Islands, her old friend and missionary colleague Mrs Charles Aurora returned to Queensland and was 'shocked to find, in this Christian land of ours, so little being done for her own people and the half-caste girls'.[25] Aurora was so distressed by the conditions that she travelled to Melbourne where she beseeched McKenzie Hatton to 'go back and help her to rescue these young and helpless girls'.[26] A letter that McKenzie Hatton wrote to Prime Minister Billy Hughes in 1921, as result of her friend's grim story, can be read as a prelude to what would eventuate some three years later. She asked for Commonwealth Government assistance to enable her 'from a moral standpoint' to look after Aboriginal girls.[27] Her communication revealed her sympathy for the horrific impact of child separation on the Aboriginal families:

> One of the saddest sights ever witnessed was the sorrow of an old man
> wailing for the loss of his little daughter, who, with no gentle hand, was
> being dragged off before his eyes by the officer of the law.[28]

In her letter she questioned the actions of the police in removing such
children: 'Where do you take these girls, and what do you do with them
when you remove them from the station?' The answer, McKenzie Hatton
reported indignantly, was that 'we take them to the city and *lose* them'.[29]
Her letter was full of the need to 'protect' and 'Christianise' Aboriginal
girls and to have 'inculcated [in them] those high ideals, which form the
basis of our civilization'. As she continued, 'no wonder some of us cry out
with longing and ask to be allowed to *save* them'.[30] But McKenzie Hatton
also praised state governments, particularly that of New South Wales, for
their efforts regarding the 'educational scheme and the generous provision'
made to Aboriginal people.[31] At this point, her argument and tone were
similar to those expressed by the majority of evangelical humanitarians of
the time.

Despite the Commonwealth Government's negative response to her
proposal, McKenzie Hatton's driving desire to establish an Aboriginal
girls' home was not to be subdued. The Australian Aborigines Mission
(AAM) newsletter the *Australian Aborigines Advocate* reported in April
1921:

> A strong Mission Council has been formed in Melbourne — Mr Thos
> Graham being President, and Mrs McKenzie-Hatton Secretary. They
> have begun work in real earnest, and already successful results have
> been achieved by our Victorian Council.[32]

Only months later, however, McKenzie Hatton cut her ties with the AAM,
soon after visiting Sydney to initiate links with the AIM. The abruptness
of this severance with the AAM in Melbourne may indicate it was not
amicable. Siding with the AIM in preference to the AAM suggests that she
had clashed with the AAM's national president, TE Colebrook, the result
of which would surface later. Colebrook carried deep-seated resentment
over the split of the New South Wales branch of the AAM thirteen years
earlier, a split that resulted in the formation of the AIM:

> For years the work of God amongst this people went on undisturbed
> by internal friction; but there came a day when the Evil One succeeded
> in creating discord, which led to the retirement of Miss Dixon, and the
> establishment of work now controlled by that lady and her husband
> (Mr. and Mrs. Long) under the name AIM or Australian [sic] Inland
> Mission. Since then the work has been carried on by two forces instead
> of one, whether with better or worse results time alone will reveal.[33]

At the centre of the split between the AAM and the AIM was missionary Retta Long and her husband LW Long.[34] Colebrook took any defection from the AAM to the AIM very badly indeed.

It was during a visit to Sydney in 1921 that McKenzie Hatton became aware of the AIM and realised that it had a similar vision to her own, that of instigating an Aboriginal girls' home. She at once offered to take up the challenge. An article in the *Melbourne Evening Herald* prematurely announced McKenzie Hatton's departure to Sydney to begin this work:

> Mrs McKenzie Hatton who has been associated with various patriotic and philanthropic schemes, leaves for Sydney to resume mission work among the half-caste girls who are in need of a motherly guardian.[35]

With a degree of perhaps unfounded optimism it was announced that 'she had been given a commission by the Aborigines Protection Board of New South Wales'.[36] Reference was drawn to her sixteen years' service in Bundaberg 'where she had a hostel for friendless half-caste girls'.[37] Her friendship to Aurora, it was revealed, was as a direct result of that hostel. Interviewed for the article, McKenzie Hatton described how she had been shocked and alarmed at the conditions young Aboriginal women faced in New South Wales: 'I find that the half-caste girl is the most neglected and degraded type I have ever encountered in my mission work'.[38]

Even at this early stage, and probably not to her benefit, McKenzie Hatton chose to criticise the Aborigines Protection Board:

> About seven years ago the Aborigines Board in New South Wales, with the idea of protecting the native girls, had an Act passed to the effect that every native girl over 14 years of age should be brought into the cities and indentured under a specially selected secretary, whose task was to find them situations in homes where they would be protected and cared for. For various reasons the scheme has not proved satisfactory.
>
> It frequently happens that the girls, tired of having been made drudges, have run away from the foster homes, and are now adrift in the cities. It is my hope that these handicapped girls, when given a chance, will be directed into a useful path of congenial service and helped toward an all round development that will assure them independence and happiness. It seems strange that large sums of money can be raised for foreign missions, but nobody seems inclined to give to the people of our own country.[39]

Her proposal was delayed when she was struck down by illness, and it was only at the end of 1923 that 'she was set free' and well enough to return to her work.[40] That November, McKenzie Hatton returned to Sydney with her three children and secured a house at Burlington Road, Homebush, to use as a home for girls. Unfortunately, the AIM had not yet gained permission from the Aborigines Protection Board to use it as such a home and, in a sign of the bitter confrontations to come, dismissed McKenzie Hatton's overture for assistance.

Unaccustomed to opposition and unaware of the Board's negativity, McKenzie Hatton remained optimistic of the Board's support and advised the AIM that she 'intended to take the place hoping that permission would be given'.[41] By January 1924, however, Hatton was facing difficulties. She had leased the house in Homebush and spent a substantial sum in furnishing it, but without the Board's approval to operate as a girls' home she was forced to break the lease and find a way of disposing of her interest in the place.[42]

Hatton soon found another home in the same street, a twelve-roomed house on large grounds. It was obvious that she fully intended to push ahead, with or without consent from the Board. The AIM endorsed the proposed use of the property and contributed £22 to assist with the first month's rent and the purchase of some furniture.[43] The first girl, Emily Melrose, was admitted and two fellow missionary women took rooms at the property to 'assist Mrs Hatton in various ways'.[44] At an official opening ceremony the home was named Rehoboth; the biblical significance of the name and the benevolent purpose of the property was given much significance in *Our Aim*:

> And he removed from thence and digged another well; for this they strove not; and he called the name of it Rehoboth; and he said, For now the Lord hath made room for us and we shall be a fruitful land.[45]

It was initially the intention of both McKenzie Hatton and the AIM that the home would not run in opposition with other missionary or government institutions, but would provide a haven for girls the Board deemed 'incorrigible'. Once labelled as such by the Board these girls were destined for institutionalisation in mental asylums or reformatories.

The opening of Rehoboth highlighted a significant early link with the future AAPA. During the ceremony 'Mr Long then called upon Miss Cora Robertson, one of our early Singleton Home Girls, to sing and with pathos and power she exhorted us in song to "Cast thy bread upon the waters"'.[46] Cora Robertson was Fred Maynard's cousin, and would later marry Sid Ridgeway, the future AAPA secretary.

The opening of Rehoboth was a great success, but only weeks later the AIM was showing the first signs of doubt in the home's activities. AIM council minutes recorded that 'should any alteration be made in the management of the Home at any time the A.I.M would be entitled to the furniture purchased with the money voted from the Home fund for that purpose'.[47]

Rehoboth Aboriginal Girls' Home, Homebush, 1924, was established by Elizabeth McKenzie Hatton. This was also the first home for the Australian Aboriginal Progressive Association.

Was this an early indication of disquiet over McKenzie Hatton's contact with Aboriginal leaders and 'agitators'?

If so, she was unaware of any misgivings on the part of the AIM.

McKenzie Hatton supported her work at Rehoboth by taking the matter of Aboriginal issues and needs to the wider public forum. In this respect she was very much a forerunner of feminist activists such as Mary Bennett, Joan Kingsley Strack and Jessica Street, all of whom rose to prominence during the 1930s.

For McKenzie Hatton, developing and fostering awareness of Aboriginal issues through the wider community was a high priority. She was in this sense more aligned with Aboriginal politics of this time than with the AIM. The Grafton *Daily Examiner* of 1926 reported that the Aboriginal leaders sought to educate and pursue the conscience of the wider public, initiating an orchestrated campaign to 'enlist the sympathy and support of the public in urging the Government to repeal the Aborigines Act as it existed on the Statute Book'.[48] The stance, objectives and argument of these Aboriginal political activists radically contravened the notions of care promoted by both the Church and government at this time. McKenzie Hatton's wider public agenda situated her solidly with this Aboriginal political argument. Aboriginal leaders argued vehemently that they were well able to look after their own affairs and families, and that they were sickened by policies and actions that continued to wrongly portray them as 'helpless children'.[49] With Aboriginal backing and direction, and by coming to know the Aboriginal communities with an intimacy that very few white people had at that time developed, McKenzie Hatton would eventually take the message of Aboriginal disadvantage to the wider populace herself. However, the results of this awakening would cause her final separation from the AIM and everything she herself had taken as gospel.

Despite the success of Rehoboth and the praise that both the home and McKenzie Hatton received in such a short space of time, opposition from within the AIM was soon being mobilised. AIM Director LW Long became unhappy with McKenzie Hatton's allegiance with the emerging Aboriginal political movement, and this was reinforced when the Board contacted Long to state that it was 'dissatisfied' with McKenzie Hatton's work.[50]

In spite of clear evidence that Rehoboth provided a caring and genuine alternative environment for Aboriginal girls, the Board demanded that one of the girls be returned to its care and be placed back into Newington Asylum! AIM's relationship with the Board was ambiguous. While the Board's Chief Protector stated that he was 'very sympathetic with the work of the Mission'[51], he was not so sympathetic with the AIM's involvement with Rehoboth.

Much of the AAM, the AIM and the Board's antipathy towards McKenzie Hatton was due to her close contact with the Aboriginal community in Sydney and beyond, and her willingness to visit the people and listen to their objections. She was informed by Retta Long of 'letters from Mr Colebrook & Miss Barker complaining that [McKenzie Hatton] had gone to La Perouse. She had promised not to go again but had done so'.[52] In spite of the tensions between the AIM and the AAM, the Longs chose to admonish McKenzie Hatton and side with Colebrook's AAM and the Board. These combined forces constituted a united front against association with Aboriginal political activists. For McKenzie Hatton the painful realisation that the Church and mission groups stood opposed to Aboriginal recovery was a stinging slap to the face. The AIM was prepared to sacrifice the genuine needs of Aboriginal people for concessions and favour, bowing down and aligning itself with the Aborigines Protection Board and its policies.

Her response was to go on the offensive, undoubtedly with the backing and support of the Aboriginal political leadership. In a defiant declaration to the AIM, McKenzie Hatton stated that 'the Homebush Home was now the centre of the "Australian Aboriginal Progressive Association"'.[53] The AIM's minutes reveal the executive's distaste that the objectives of the

AAPA 'appeared to be purely political and social'.[54] McKenzie Hatton's defiant stance prompted a disciplinary interview, the result of which was a mutual severance between the home and the AIM:

> The ... mission disassociated itself entirely from Mrs Hatton's present activities. Resolved that Mrs Hatton be informed that the objects of the Home as present conducted, being altogether different from those of the Mission and that for which it was instigated. We withdraw all support and sever all connection with the Home.[55]

By severing its ties with McKenzie Hatton and going on to inform the Board, the AIM let loose a pack of hounds baying for blood. The Board quickly instigated an investigation into McKenzie Hatton's background and implemented directives to make life as difficult as possible for her and the Aboriginal political activists with whom she had aligned herself. The Board secretary, AC Pettitt, requested information from Victorian counterparts regarding her activities 'amongst natives in Victoria'.[56] They called for police surveillance and a report on the activities of the girls' home, a clear attempt at intimidation.[57] For Aboriginal people during this period, such rules, regulations and restrictions were representative of a strictly enforced police state. But in a clear act of her continuing rebellion, and despite attempted intimidation, McKenzie Hatton contacted the Board seeking approval to visit the Aboriginal reserves it controlled. These requests were not approved.[58]

The AIM placed a thinly disguised rebuke of McKenzie Hatton and her activities in the next issue of *Our Aim*, officially announcing its severance:

> Our readers will no doubt remember that early last year an Aboriginal Girls Home was opened and named 'Rehoboth' at Burlington Road, Homebush. Mrs Hatton some months ago felt led to introduce other work into the Home which quickly changed its character, and has finally resolved itself into an Aboriginal Institute, and is the present headquarters of an 'Aboriginal Progressive Association' for both men and women, having for its object the social betterment of the people. The A.I.M. Council, who considering that the Home no longer came under the specific object of the A.I.M., viz., the evangelization of the aboriginal races of Australia, passed a resolution severing our connection.[59]

The period when the Aboriginal political leaders had been somewhat hidden from public view was now over. As a white woman, McKenzie Hatton had been able to pursue their agenda with a degree of secrecy. It could be argued, perhaps, that McKenzie Hatton had to this moment been used as a public front by the imaginative and committed campaigners of the AAPA. Quite clearly, there were things a white person — especially a white woman — could achieve on the quiet, things that were well outside the possibilities for Aboriginal people to achieve themselves.

The events at Rehoboth were part of a rising Aboriginal political movement, and the Board soon began to feel the heat of the public's gaze for virtually the first time through media scrutiny. In late 1924 and into 1925 the influential and widely read *Sydney Morning Herald* and the *Sun* both gave concerted coverage to the issues of Aboriginal reserves, separation of 'half-caste' children and the overall future of Aboriginal people. On 29 October 1924 the *Sydney Morning Herald* ran a story that drew attention to the fact that Aboriginal girls were being denied any chance of marriage. The article drew the public's attention to the well-publicised and argued theory that Aboriginal people were a doomed and disappearing race. The journalist raised the question: if this was the unavoidable climax of white colonisation, should the actions of the Board itself accelerate this process?

> The answer of course must be no. Yet, if the system introduced a few years ago ... is allowed to continue, there cannot, very few years hence, be many Aboriginal children ... This system, which aims at the segregation of the sexes, is making it difficult for many more to be born. [60]

In what was probably a direct Board response to this criticism a commentator in the editorial section replied:

> No problem in connection with our Aboriginal race is more difficult than that concerning the girls. It is unfair to leave them on the reserves, where it is almost impossible to keep them out of the reach of white undesirables. The Aborigines Protection Board arranges for a preliminary training in domestic work on the reserves, and then distributes them among suitable white households, where their training as useful members of the community is completed. [61]

The writer unknowingly and with chilling precision went on to disclose the real agenda behind such a practice: 'The teaching of anthropology indicates that in a generation or two the full-bloods in this State will have vanished and that somewhat later the half-caste will be merged into the dominant white race'. [62] But in an article written earlier, one Annie Bowden — an Aboriginal woman from La Perouse — presented a differing viewpoint of the place of Aboriginal women:

> The women were always taken care of in my case, and made much of, there was more discipline in the camps than there is in many white homes today... Boys were taught from earliest infancy to respect their

mothers and their sisters, and no one woman had more than one husband.[63]

Bowden's article is significant on a number of fronts, as it presents an Aboriginal viewpoint in total opposition to the so-called white authority on Aboriginal issues. She attacked an article written by Daisy Bates in the *Sydney Morning Herald* with venom. It was indeed rare that an Aboriginal voice was given the opportunity of being heard in such mass media outlets. Bowden challenged the viewpoint of Bates over Aboriginal language:

> She states that all Aboriginal dialects throughout Australia have terms only for the lowest, such as lying and cheating and thieving, and no terms honesty, making the language in common with the rest as low as she possibly can. It would be laughable if it were not so serious; and we know it is not true. I am an aboriginal and understand and speak eight different languages. I am an educated woman, having been educated in the State schools of Victoria and I think I am in a better position to know than a white woman.[64]

Bowden ridiculed Bates's assertion of Aboriginal cannibalism and claims of witnessing Aboriginal initiation ceremonies, and with perfect clarity articulated the obstacles that stood before Aboriginal people and hopes for political voice:

> There are at the present time many aboriginal men in Australia, dark and half-caste, that would gladly do anything to better themselves and if possible get into public positions, if they were not barred by the White Australia policy. What chance has a black man got of trying to raise himself? No matter how he tried to lift himself up he would still be classed as one of the undesirables.[65]

In the face of this media barrage, and the pressures caused by the now oppositional Rehoboth girls' home, the Board was at a loss for a while about what action it should take in response. In early January 1925 the issue was back on the pages of the *Sydney Morning Herald* when the paper drew the public's attention to the extreme cruelty to parents and relatives through the Board's child-removal policy. In Grafton a well-respected Aboriginal mother and father had their four young children — all under thirteen years of age — taken from them just prior to Christmas. A local councillor, J N Short, was indignant at the Board's action:

> He said the parents had come to him about their trouble, and he went with the father to the police officer. It appeared that the officer's instructions [by the Board] were to meet the children at the ferry, and thither they went accompanied by their parents, who did not know that their little ones were to be taken away from them. The scene at the parting was heart rending, but the children were taken, despite protests

and tears, and conveyed to Kempsey. The children had been properly fed and clothed by the parents. It was a nice Christmas box to give to the parents of the children — to wrest their children from them. The parents were in a terrible state about it, and were calling at his place every day asking him when they were to have their little ones back. [66]

The paper exonerated the police of any guilt in the matter, disclosing that the action taken to remove the children was as a result of a directive given by the Aborigines Protection Board. It also went on to credit the mother as one with a fine reputation as a hard-working and honest individual, and it was noted that 'residents in the vicinity of the Grafton reserve are said to be empathetic on the point that the children were not neglected, and a petition urging the return of the children to the care of their parents is being prepared for presentation to the authorities'.[67]

The Board was on the defensive through the embarrassing exposures in the press. But they were now fully alerted and were preparing to unleash the full extent of their powers upon both McKenzie Hatton and the Aboriginal leadership of the AAPA.

While McKenzie Hatton was proving to be a thorn in the Board's side in Sydney, John Moloney's *Voice of the North* newspaper was the focus of dissent in Newcastle and the New South Wales mid-north coast. As editor of the Newcastle newspaper, Moloney maintained a consistent campaign of editorials about Aboriginal people and issues. Having travelled widely in Europe, the Middle East, New Zealand and the Pacific, Moloney developed a broad appreciation of other cultures. In the Newcastle area he fostered contact with Aboriginal people, including those at the reserve at Karuah. The AIM newsletter *Our AIM* reported:

> We were favoured with a visit from our old friend Mr Moloney, of Newcastle, who bought with him Mr David Unaipon a full-blood Aboriginal from South Australia. We gathered our people together in the church, which was again full. After some singing and playing on the lawn by the children. We listened with interest to addresses by Mr Moloney and Mr Unaipon.[68]

While we memorialise David Unaipon today through his image on the Australian fifty-dollar note, most Australians remain totally unaware of his achievements as a writer, inventor and public speaker. Unaipon asserted some indirect influence over the AAPA platform, stating in 1922 that 'every Australian Aboriginal should have his own farm or garden in fee simple, and be permitted to rear his own family in his own way. The argument is incontrovertible'.[69] Two years later this statement was taken up word for word by the AAPA in its fight for land and children.

During the early 1920s Moloney attended WEA classes conducted in the Hunter Valley by the then little-known AP Elkin on the subject of Aboriginal culture and society.[70] This study added to Moloney's already fierce nationalism. He was a member of the Australian Natives Association and was the foundation secretary of the Australasian Society of Patriots (ASP), an organisation whose membership was confined to people born in 'Australia, New Zealand, Tasmania or any of the islands in the Pacific Ocean South of the Equator'.[71]

In 1917 the ASP proposed a fanciful 'Noah's ark' venture on Bulba Island in Lake Macquarie. The island was to be stocked with native flora and fauna 'as was observed by Captain Cook when he discovered Australia', and the ASP 'aspired to transform the island into 'a miniature Australia', and several Aboriginal families were to be encouraged to settle there.[72]

Up to 1922 Moloney's understanding of Aboriginal people and issues was somewhat patronising, and not unlike many other humanitarians of the time. Like McKenzie Hatton, it was his meeting and association with Aboriginal leaders such as Fred Maynard, Tom Lacey and Sid Ridgeway that marked a great shift in his view and motives. His comments in the *Voice of the North* vividly presented the crimes of Australia's recent past, and he criticised the role that the construction of history played in the continued dispossession of Aboriginal people:

> The treatment of the native people of Australia is a black blot on our national history ... The defamation of the aboriginals is, in a large measure, traceable to the lessons contained in the school books which were imported for use in the Australian schools more than two generations ago. If the books for use in Australian schools had been written in Australia by Australians, at the dawn of our Education System, things might have been vastly different today.[73]

It was around this time that the tone of the coverage in the *Voice of the North* began a subtle but distinct shift from the romanticised view of saving Aboriginal people to a more politically attuned view. Moloney was quick to recognise and listen to the Aboriginal voice. He gave press coverage to a group of Hunter Valley Kooris who were drawing attention to the fact that the Aboriginal Protection Board had implemented a systematic program of stripping Aboriginal peoples of their land and children.

The year 1924 through to 1925 had witnessed some groundbreaking initiatives and developments in Aboriginal issues: the establishment of Rehoboth and the subsequent defection of Elizabeth McKenzie Hatton to the Aboriginal cause; the support of JJ Moloney and coverage in his newspaper the *Voice of the North*; and the public exposure and embarrassment suffered by the New South Wales Aborigines Protection

Board in major newspapers over its practice of removing Aboriginal children from their families. The seeds that had been sown and developed over years of hardship by Aboriginal people were now ready to flower.

***

Into this arena of hostility and confrontation, and into the public gaze for the first time, stepped the members of the Australian Aboriginal Progressive Association. Despite the Board holding all of the aces, the AAPA set about taking advantage of every way and means to embarrass and attack the stupidity of the Board's actions. As a result the AAPA was instantly front-page news in Sydney.

The AAPA's first conference was held in St David's Hall, Surry Hills. Newspaper headlines immediately trumpeted 'On Aborigines Aspirations — First Australians To Help Themselves — Self Determination' and 'Aborigines In Conference — Self Determination Is Their Aim – To Help A People'.[74] President Fred Maynard began proceedings with the call 'Brothers and sisters, we have much business to transact so let's get right down to it'.[75] Over two hundred enthusiastic Aboriginal people were in attendance and 'they heartily supported the objectives of the association'.[76] Maynard wasted no time in outlining the AAPA's directives, and his inaugural address rang with the influences of Marcus Garvey:

St Davids Church and hall in Surry Hills. The was the site of the inaugural AAPA conference in April 1925; the first Australian Aboriginal civil rights convention.

> We aim at the spiritual, political, industrial and social. We want to work out our own destiny. Our people have not had the courage to stand together in the past, but now we are united, and are determined to work for the preservation for all of those interests which are near and dear to us. [77]

The *Daily Guardian* highlighted the large cross-section of the Aboriginal community present: 'the old and young were there. The well-dressed matronly woman and the shingled girl of 19. The old man of 60 and the young man of athletic build. All are fighting for the preservation of the rights of aborigines for self-determination.[78]

Maynard declared that 'Aboriginal people were sufficiently advanced in the sciences to control their own affairs'.[79] Elizabeth McKenzie Hatton was one of the conference convenors and welcomed the Aboriginal delegates, many of whom had journeyed from various parts of the state in order to read papers on the conditions at many of the Aboriginal reserves in New South Wales. She stressed that 'aboriginal interests had suffered in the past from lack of organisation'.[80] Delegates recorded the grave state of conditions that existed on the reserves. One delegate cried that 'Conditions for Greeks and Italians are far better than those applying to our own people'.[81] Reference was made to the fact that Aboriginal people were suffering due to the encroachment of 'foreigners' onto what had strictly been areas of Aboriginal labour. Aboriginal people were being pushed back and away from work now given over to others for oyster and fishing leases. [82]

In response to a vote of thanks put forth by the AAPA and delegates for her recent enlistment drive to Kempsey, Grafton, and other locations throughout the state, McKenzie Hatton responded with a clear call to arms:

> There was a definite need for an Aborigines 'Wake-Up' Movement. I came over here from another State expecting to preach to heathen people. But I found an eager, keen people who demanded a voice in their own destiny. You have come through the fires of persecution, insult and opposition. You refused to be pushed out of your own country, which is that of your fathers … I am delighted to see in you a spirit of pride in your own country. This association is for uplift, spiritually and socially. It is progressive in policy. We feel that your best interests have not been considered. The Government has no policy for your industrial development.[83]

Hatton's speech revealed that 'branches of the association are being formed in the country centres. We are not a rich body but we feel sure that well-meaning citizens will come to our financial assistance'.[84] It was noted that the organisation had already obtained a membership in excess of five hundred. The conference went on to discuss matters of cooperation, migration and other actions that were calculated to benefit Aboriginal people.[85] The conference was a resounding success and the Aboriginal people in attendance went back to their communities fired with resolve. It signified blatant rebellion and a clear challenge to the Board and the authority it exerted over Aboriginal people and their lives.

The imprint of Garveyism was deeply embedded in the platform of the new movement. The logo, motto and much of the political rhetoric of the AAPA were incorporated from the doctrine of Garvey and his group, the Universal Negro Improvement Association. The clarion call of Garvey's UNIA was 'One God! One Aim! One Destiny!',[86] the same as the AAPA. In his poem *Africa for the Africans* Garvey cried:

> Europe Cries to Europeans. Ho!
> Asiatics claim Asia, so
> Australia for Australians
> And Africa for Africans

'Australia for Australians' was the battle cry featured on the AAPA logo: surely no coincidence. In his manifesto Garvey wrote 'We are organised for the absolute purpose of bettering our condition, industrially, commercially, socially, religiously and politically'.[87]

In its four years in the public spotlight the AAPA would make continued demands through the media. There were frequent statements by Fred Maynard that the AAPA encouraged Aboriginal self-respect through spiritual, political, industrial and social ideals. The Aboriginal political movement was now charged with enthusiasm for enforcing government change to Aboriginal affairs.

5.

The Rise and Impact of the 'Freedom Club'

We are always coming up with the emphatic facts of history in our private experience and verifying them here. All history becomes subjective, in other words there is properly no history, only biography.

Ralph Waldo Emerson

The New South Wales Aborigines Protection Board was about to be brought to full awareness that the Aboriginal political movement was no flash in the pan. On one of its trips to the New South Wales north coast in early 1925, Elizabeth McKenzie Hatton — with the aid of the Nambucca Heads community — removed an Aboriginal girl, Eileen Buchanan, from the Board's control.[1] The Board, infuriated and driven to desperate measures, called on the Crown Solicitor for advice on how to deal with this challenge to its control. In calling on the Crown Solicitor the Board sought to ascertain what powers it had 'to deal with the activities of Mrs Hatton of Homebush'.[2] The matter was specifically placed in the hands of the Inspector General of Police — who was also chair of the Aborigines Protection Board.[3] However, in a complete endorsement of the AAPA's actions the Crown Solicitor informed the Board that it could undertake no action against McKenzie Hatton or the AAPA.[4]

Such success in openly defying the Board had an inspiring impact on the Aboriginal community. Throughout this period the AAPA received many impassioned pleas for assistance and sought at every opportunity to assist their people in their fight for social justice. 'One man wrote from a far-back settlement, asking that someone should come and tell them about the "Freedom Club"'.[5] A journalist, reporting in the *Macleay Argus* in April 1925, highlighted the well-orchestrated recruitment drive of the

AAPA in enlisting support within the Kempsey district. He began the article with his perception of the local white population's prejudiced view of the local Aboriginal people and dominant attitude towards them:

> The coloured people of the district are looked upon in a general way by the man about the street as a kind of nuisance. He says they are necessary for the simple reason that they cannot disappear altogether at the word of command, and a nuisance because, well, they're coloured. The aboriginal cannot help but see this attitude towards him ... It has also been recognised, too, that ordinary preaching and missionary work is looked upon by the coloured people with suspicion in as much, that they soon see they are classed as heathen and in want of pity.[6]

The report went on to note the arrival in Kempsey of McKenzie Hatton. The reporter highlighted that she stressed that the current government directives were totally wrong and achieved nothing in improving Aboriginal conditions. She was supported by a strong and determined committee of Aboriginal people who were totally committed to the complete overthrow of these ineffective policies that appeared to encourage the disappearance of Aboriginal people and culture instead of providing any means of hope or protection in a real sense. These unjust government methods encouraged and enforced the status quo and were completely out of touch with the reality and dilemma of the Aboriginal situation. McKenzie Hatton and the AAPA had a different agenda and intended to 'alter the whole thing and try not to preach to the aboriginal as if he were something harmless and in want of pity and help, but as a clear minded citizen requiring a little different treatment to the ordinary citizen'.[7]

The journalist revealed that, although in its infancy, the AAPA had caught on particularly well among Aboriginal people. Aboriginal people had rallied to support and join the fledgling organisation and branches had sprung up in many districts. Attention was directed to the fact that the AAPA had recently held a conference in Sydney 'entirely run by the aboriginals themselves — chairman, secretary and treasurer included — and even the business paper was the work of these people'.[8] McKenzie Hatton arrived in Kempsey and began a recruiting campaign at the local showground. A large number of Aboriginal people attended this meeting 'at which Mrs Hatton explained the aims and methods of the AAPA'.[9] Attention was given to the fact that this remarkable meeting was highly significant because of the large attendance of so many of the 'very old aborigines of this district, old identities of the Macleay River. They were as keen as any in the movement and these old veterans were called upon to speak at the close of the address of the lady who had come to organise the work here'.[10]

The significance of the presence of respected and well-known Aboriginal elders such as James Linwood and John Mosely cannot be overemphasised, nor can their decision to conduct much of their address in Aboriginal language. The act of speaking in Aboriginal language clearly grounded the importance of maintaining and asserting their cultural identity in the framework and direction of this new organisation. In light of this, local elder Reuben Kelly recalled of Fred Maynard that 'he spoke in perfect English, and was good in his own tongue as well'.[11] Elder Linwood delivered his address 'in the aboriginal language', and strongly urged the local Aboriginal people to join the AAPA and:

> Work together in the interests of their own race. He referred to the unjust procedure of late years, when many of them after years of occupancy of certain portions of land, and after clearing it, and cultivating it, had been turned adrift to begin all over again in some unwanted portion of the country'.[12]

Linwood was given a rousing reception and loudly applauded as he touched on the issues that were central and of great concern to so many of the Aboriginal people present. In his address John Moseley also urged the large gathering to join the AAPA.

Capitalising on the day's success, a large meeting was conducted in the Salvation Army Hall that evening. The local Salvation Army had generously loaned the hall to the AAPA, and in this they showed some direct but discreet support. The hall was jam-packed, and again the significant local Aboriginal elders occupied the front seats. Elizabeth McKenzie Hatton delivered a passionate address in an inspirational and rallying tone. She 'urged them to wake from the long dream of centuries'.[13] She was forthright that the Aboriginal dilemma was as a direct consequence of both government bungling and sinister objective:

> The greatest hindrance to the welfare of these people was the system so long in vogue of handing out rations to the people and nursing them; these people were well able to work and support their own families and the AAPA was out to teach the people self-respect, and that could only be brought about when they took on the responsibility of their own support and development.[14]

Thus, the AAPA represented everything that Aboriginal people had hoped for and been denied. They now stood defiantly before the government in total opposition to its policy towards Aboriginal people. The AAPA offered hope and a genuine alternative. This group was an all-Aboriginal organisation and, importantly, reflected Aboriginal recognition and directive in taking control of their own lives and affairs.

It was for Aboriginals. It was progressive and aimed to lift the Aboriginal people in every way, spiritually, socially and industrially. It was an association, which suggested that they must pull together for the good of all.[15]

The report described the president, Fred Maynard, as 'a coloured man, who ... followed Mrs Hatton, and he urged the people to join the AAPA and to remember that when joining they were responsible for the honour of the association'.[16] The journalist noted that '[Maynard] gave a splendid recitation at the close of his speech entitled "The Other Fellow", which was warmly appreciated'.[17]

Maynard's paper deserves greater scrutiny. The original paper on which the address was based does not survive, but the title mentioned in the press report, 'The Other Fellow', certainly has a strong post-colonial ring to it. It takes little imagination to realise to whom Maynard was referring. Aboriginal people during this period were strategically categorised as the maligned and marginalised 'other'. In recent decades post-colonial theory has drawn greater historical recognition of the nature of the colonial past in defining the oppressed 'other'.

It is amazing that an Aboriginal man had preceded by decades this line of thought and argument on the way society had practised its forms of exclusion. Maynard's paper demonstrates that he was not about to wait, be asked or invited to speak but recognised the importance of not remaining as the silenced other. In contrast, decades ahead of his time and thinking, he was bent on drawing attention to the process of marginalisation and giving full voice to this 'other fellow'.

This understanding of the articulate and well read Maynard again draws uncanny comparisons with Marcus Garvey. In a 1922 paper delivered in New York Garvey had forcefully declared:

> We represent a new line of thought among Negroes. Whether you call it advanced thought or reactionary thought, I do not care. If it is reactionary for people to seek independence in government, then we are reactionary. If it is advanced thought for people to seek liberty and freedom, then we represent the advanced school of thought among the Negroes of this country. We of the U.N.I.A. believe that what is good for the *other fellow* is good for us. If government is something that is worth while; if government is something that is appreciable and helpful and protective to others, then we also want to experiment in government. We do not mean a government that will make us citizens without rights or subjects without consideration. We mean the kind of government that will place our race in control...[18]

Both Maynard and Garvey were powerful and inspiring speakers, as young men they had carried and studied a dictionary to improve their vocabulary, and both had a great appreciation of Ralph Waldo Emerson. Speaking at Kempsey, Maynard quoted Emerson: 'If a man built a better house or even a better mouse trap than the other man, though he be in the dense woods the world would make a beaten track to his door'.[19] For his part, Garvey 'preached with telling force and earnestness Emerson's gospel of self-reliance' and William H Ferris, editor of the *Negro World*, averred that 'there is something in Emerson's advice to "hitch your wagon to a star", which was undoubtedly the same inspiration as the advice that Garvey used in his exhortation to "lift up yourselves men, take yourselves out of the mire and hitch your hopes to the stars; yes, rise as high as the very stars themselves"'.[20]

At the conclusion of the evening James Linwood and John Moseley rose and proposed a vote of thanks to McKenzie Hatton on the success of the campaign, which had already witnessed the recruitment of another one hundred members to the AAPA.[21]

The methods employed by the AAPA in gaining widespread media coverage were all about breaking the process of marginalisation and injustice. Its achievements in this process are widely evident. In May 1925 the *Daily Guardian* reported the callous policy employed by the Board in forcing Aboriginal people from their hard-worked-for and cultivated land. The much-respected elder Jimmy Linwood was being forced to leave his beloved farm on the Fattorini Island of the Macleay Valley[22] after over three decades of toil. It was little wonder that Linwood elected to join the AAPA, and he had vented his anger and frustration from the podium only days before. He was obviously well aware of the developments to rip his land away in a totally unfair manner.

The *Guardian*'s account highlighted the injustice inflicted upon Linwood and clearly portrayed the Board and the Lands department as the guilty parties. The headline banner declared 'Is It Fair To Aborigines? — Lands Department is Materialistic — Selling Patarone [sic]'.[23] The article went on to cry for justice:

> Will the people of NSW stand by and see the aborigines ejected from their beautiful Patarone Island? It has been theirs since the days of antiquity. So have the adjoining rich river flats. But with the advent of the white settler, the aboriginal has gradually been forced to occupy odd bits of reservation land. Now a cruel materialistic Lands Department has decreed that the island shall be sold.[24]

Attention was drawn to what was described as a pathetic and futile protest by the 'chief' of the once powerful tribe, Jimmy Linwood, to halt the land sale process. Linwood and his family were noted as being totally devoted to the island, land on which they had worked and prospered. Attention was drawn to the fact that the Linwoods had shipped as much as four hundred bags of maize annually. For no reason other than that others now wanted their land, the Aboriginal inhabitants had been removed by force by the local police. Ted Moran, another Aboriginal farmer, was described as having died of a broken heart as a result of the injustice of having his land stripped away. Linwood, his wife and eleven children had suffered immeasurably from the eviction and were depicted as social wrecks.[25]

It was acknowledged in the press that at this late hour 'Elizabeth McKenzie Hatton of the Australian Aboriginal Progressive Association' had arrived in an attempt to save the island and land for the original owners.[26] Seven days later another report in the *Guardian* highlighted an attempt by the Board to quell any hope of public sympathy and support for the Aboriginal protest. Inspector Robert Donaldson, the Board's spokesman, supported the Lands department's push for the land. Donaldson had a sinister and foreboding reputation among Aboriginal people because of his decades of work with the Board, gaining the frightening name and reputation as the 'kids collector'.[27] As far back as 1909 he was writing reports for the Board on the importance of gaining greater authority to take Aboriginal kids from their families. It appears to have become Donaldson's life mission to break down Aboriginal people and communities. He saw and sought no redeeming qualities in Aboriginal people or culture. It was, therefore, understandable that this man now tried to belittle 'Mrs McKenzie-Hatton's protest on behalf of the natives'.[28] Falsely describing the island as neglected, Donaldson said that it had 'of late become a sanctuary for undesirables owing to its isolation and its thick undergrowth'.[29]

An analysis of John Mosely and Jimmy Linwood's stories, however, delivers a vastly different picture. These two Aboriginal men were originally given approval to farm on the Fattorini Islands in the Macleay River in 1883.[30] The Board's report of that year claimed that there was no open country on the islands, that they were poorly grassed and had been partly cleared and cropped with maize. The islands were in fact heavily timbered and full of scrub. Linwood and his sons worked tirelessly in backbreaking and humid conditions to clear their land ready for cultivation and stock. By 1889 there had been an amazing turn around: Linwood had three homes, two ploughs and one harrow and his return on his maize crop of £156/0/8 had seen him rise out of debt.[31] Linwood even took first prize in the Kempsey show with the quality of his maize.[32] The properties had highly productive gardens and vegetable crops which included corn, potatoes, beans, cabbages, peas, pumpkins and melons.[33]

Incredibly, the information the Board had at its disposal at the time strongly reflected decades of success that Aboriginal farmers were achieving on the land. A reporter in the *Australian Aborigines Advocate* in 1915 recorded that 'I would like to note the way in which Moran's and Linwood's land was being cultivated, and the industry displayed in both cases, as being most credible to these men.'[34]

Even more telling is a report from the Board Inspector himself:

> As late as August 1919, Board Inspector, HL Swindlehurst had emphatically advised against revocation of the two Fattorini Islands and Pelican Island on the grounds that the Guri residents were farming the land effectively.[35]

Aboriginal farmers had a long and widespread history of success. There were several significant land grants made available for Aboriginal people between 1890 and 1909. According to Goodall, 'At the height of Aboriginal holding of reserve lands in 1911, there were 115 reserves totalling 26,000 acres. Of these, 75 were created on Aboriginal initiative'.[36] In many cases these were independent reserves or farm holdings, and life on these holdings was a complete contrast to the stifling conditions of reserve life that were to come after 1909 as part of the New South Wales Aborigines Protection Board policy. Aboriginal knowledge of their land and environment usually ensured that farming successes marked these independent land holdings.

The downturn came with the encroachment and envy of white settlement, followed shortly thereafter with the introduction of the First World War Soldier Settlement Scheme, which drew allotments — particularly from Aboriginal reserve land. This directive allowed returned servicemen access to land for housing, farming and development. The Aboriginal farming land was seen as prime cleared and cultivated land. 'In fact, a number of Aboriginal reserves were revoked or reduced in size so that the land could be allotted to returned soldiers under the Soldier Settlement Scheme'.[37]

There were many successes noted on the New South Wales north coast 'of the "industriousness" of Aboriginal farmers on Pelican Island, Kinchela and other reserves'.[38] The Board itself gave testimony to Aboriginal farming success, describing Aboriginal land holdings:

> They are all cleared and cultivated, maize being chiefly grown. On the whole the Aborigines are in a flourishing condition, having horses and sulkies of their own. They have also provided themselves with boats.[39]

At Arakoon, at the mouth of the Macleay River, 'three Aborigines were reported to have been cultivating vacant land well before 1883, the police commented: Aboriginals are very proud of calling a piece of ground their own'.[40] Another case on the Clarence River, at Ulgundaha [sic] Island revealed that the Aboriginal families had:

> Been doing well with their plots lately and several have already secured substantial returns. Two families who cultivated under an acre of land shipped 30 bags of beans in three shipments; this has returned them a cheque of £103 for their labour, and only for the unsettled weather conditions they would have been able to ship a further 100 bags from the island. There are nine families living on the island and they are well contented with their lot.[41]

Despite the overwhelming evidence available to it, the Board forced Aboriginal people off these farms with literally only the clothes they had on their backs. They received nothing for decades of effort, sweat and tears. In a final cruel irony the nature of their removal was recognised decades later, but that recognition only came with the passing of legislation to protect the government from legal challenge over the wrongs of the past:

> Ironically, it became clear in the 1970s that ALL of these revocations were in fact illegal, a problem solved by the Wran Government by passing legislation concurrently with its 1983 *Land Rights Act* which retrospectively validated the second dispossession.[42]

Although unable to halt the process of the stripping away of the Fattorini Island from the Linwood family, the anger, frustration and indignation Aboriginal people felt towards the Board now burned with a white-hot glow. There were 192 applicants for Linwood's land; it was eventually sold off to a local farmer for £55 per acre.[43]

The AAPA and its supporters responded and used every opportunity through the media to target the Board and its insidious methods of dispossession. In recent years there has been a strong push for an investigation of missing Aboriginal trust funds. This may well be just the tip of an iceberg. What happened to the money received for the Aboriginal farming land? It has been estimated that some 13,000 acres was revoked and, if it was valued at £50 an acre (as some evidence indicates), that equates to £650,000 — an incredible sum by today's standards.

***

In articles in the *Wingham Chronicle* and Newcastle's *Voice of the North* it was reported that Elizabeth McKenzie Hatton declared she had first come over to New South Wales from Victoria in an attempt to understand the 'apathy and hopelessness which seemed to be the habitual condition of the aboriginal people'.[44] She indicated that at first she did not doubt that the New South Wales government had honourable intentions in its actions and directives with regard to its Aboriginal population. However, she soon recognised that despite attempts by many well-intentioned missionary workers the Aboriginal people were in a state of complete and enforced hopelessness. 'I have just returned from my third visit along the North Coast Line, where I have visited the camps and settlements of the aboriginal people'.[45] McKenzie Hatton was quick to illustrate the proliferation of wealth of the white population within these districts at the expense of the Aboriginal people, and did not hide her contempt:

> Signs of prosperity all around. I have visited the different shows everywhere I heard of record cattle and horses, splendid results in the culture of every known product; wealth evidenced by the motors, and well dressed people with money to burn. Oh! This marvellous North Coast country. I revelled in the magnificence of its possibilities. I am an Australian, and oh! How glorious is our heritage; but all the time the horror of the thought of our injustice to the wretched people who originally owned this land. What have we done for them?[46]

The experience of the Linwood family, and many others suffering similarly through the revocation of their farms, had a direct influence on McKenzie Hatton's actions. Across the state she and the officials of the AAPA discovered Aboriginal people thrown from their homes and fenced off from years of labour and effort with absolutely no support, compensation or opportunity to challenge these consequences. Land which had been supposedly reserved for them was ruthlessly stripped away. The land was then:

> sold to the highest bidder, or leased to white people, already made wealthy by using the labour of these poor coloured people devoid of equitable recourse ... They have come through the fires of persecution and ill-treatment, and have reached a stage when with a little help and encouragement they could be made more useful citizens.[47]

The number of forced expulsions had escalated during recent months, the result of which was incredible hardship for the Aboriginal community:

> The land is being sold, and they are finding themselves on the roadsides, or any corner of 'no man's land' where they, in their hapless lot find themselves, homeless, disheartened, and resentful at the injustice which is being meted out to them.[48]

McKenzie Hatton trumpeted the formation of the AAPA, its platform and the critical issues which it sought to bring to the public's attention. She strongly grounded the AAPA stance, which had two main objectives:

First – That the aboriginal will be given a small portion of land and his own right to build his home upon. A five acre or ten acre lot is asked for in a suitable location.

Second – They beg that their homes will no longer be despoiled; but that they may be allowed to keep their children with them and develop them along the lines of their own initiative. They are both very modest requests, which every fair-minded Australian would readily support.[49]

In conclusion, Elizabeth McKenzie Hatton highlighted once more the horrific experiences that confronted Aboriginal people and revealed the simmering anger held by the Aboriginal population with regard to those who were supposedly making decisions in their best interests. In total contradiction of government propaganda that Aboriginal parents did not care for their children and soon forgot they existed once taken away, the AAPA received an avalanche of correspondence begging for help:

Day after day letters come from the people, pleading for their children, asking me to find the girls, long lost to them — in service somewhere in this State — taken away in some cases over seven years ago and no word or line from them. Surely we can do better for these people than this [yet] in our abominable selfishness still we endeavour to filch the last remaining crumbs from the aboriginal people.[50]

As well as reasserting Aboriginal people's prior ownership and overriding right to land, McKenzie Hatton used every opportunity to articulate Aboriginal communities' horror of the Board's child-removal policy. Records from as far back as 1912 reveal that Aboriginal people at Old Burnt Bridge and Rollands Plains reserves sent petitions of complaint to the New South Wales Aborigines Protection Board stating their objection to the action of 'taking away young children from the reserves.[51]

The Board's response, especially after the 1909 Act and its more far-reaching amendment in 1915, was to try and break Aboriginal resolve — especially regarding the removal of children. In an interview many years later Jack Campbell recalled his near miss with being taken from his parents. After receiving an earlier warning that the Board's Inspector Donaldson was about and looking to 'kidnap kids' his parents kept him home from the reserve school. This did not deter Donaldson, who approached the Campbells' house:

Jack's mother fired a shotgun over Donaldson's head, sending him back into Kempsey to fetch the police. It was clearly imperative for the family to escape the district altogether after the incident and so the Campbells went south down the coast in Jack's father's fishing boat.[52]

The Campbells became refugees in their own country, taking up residence in the Saltpan Creek camp in Sydney. Similar events occurred throughout the state:

> In two separate incidents on Burnt Bridge fathers resorted to threats of violence to protect their children from the predications of the Board. On both occasions the Boards Officers were threatened with guns. As one incident was recounted, 'Old DC ... he had a fair mob of kids. This bloke [Board officer] had em in a car or something to take em. [The Board officer] had em and [DC] pulled a shotgun. 'Let the kids go,' he said 'or I'll blow you over'. He let em out ... On another occasion a similar exchange occurred between a particular Board Officer, Donaldson, and a Burnt Bridge farmer, old Mr D. said to Donaldson, 'I know what'll stop you' He was going away and Mr Donaldson looked back like that and said 'What'? He [D.] said, 'a lump of lead'. He never came back anymore. He [D.] wasn't frightened at all.[53]

By mid 1925 a well-justified AAPA protest against the Board and its policies was well under way. Illustrating powerfully the AAPA's ability to generate widespread headline-grabbing attention, reports in the Sydney *Daily Guardian,* Newcastle's *Voice of the North,* Kempsey's *Macleay Chronicle* and *Macleay Argus* and Wingham's *Wingham Chronicle and Manning River Observer* reported the half-yearly meeting of the AAPA conducted at St David's Hall in Surry Hills, Sydney, in July 1925.[54]

These articles highlight the impressive organisational structures established by the AAPA and the fact that Aboriginal people attended the half-yearly meeting in force, taking 'a lively interest in proceedings'.[55] Described by the *Macleay Chronicle* as 'a coloured man of exceptional ability', AAPA president Fred Maynard was scathing and informative on the detrimental government policies regarding Aboriginal affairs.[56] Newspaper reports show that, at the time of the meeting, the AAPA was in the process of establishing offices in Sydney to allow it to best deal with the appeals and needs of its people. Indications were made that they would approach the government in seeking funds to assist in this process. Maynard once more used the opportunity to highlight the absurdity of the Aborigines Act and the policies directed at Aboriginal people:

> "One thing we want to see", said Maynard "is the repeal of the Aborigines Act. To allow such an Act to remain on the Statute Book is not only an absurdity, but an insult to the aborigines of the country. It might have been alright when Parliament passed it, but it has outlived its usefulness. Fancy in these days of progress and enlightenment an Act in operation which provides that the aborigines shall receive a

pinch of sugar, tea and flour. There are many clauses which are now objectionable, and if we can awaken the public conscience we hope to have them removed".[57]

Maynard went on to highlight the incredible response from Aboriginal communities to the AAPA. He stated that, having recently returned to Sydney after trips to some outback centres, 'it simply amazes me to see the interest the people are taking in this movement'.[58] He went on to make an appreciative statement about the work and commitment put in by Elizabeth McKenzie Hatton which reveals the difficulties that she, Maynard and the other office bearers of the AAPA faced. The main difficulty was denial of access to Aboriginal reserves, an enforced directive of the Board. McKenzie Hatton and the AAPA's leaders had no access to enter Aboriginal reserves. This did little to stifle the flow of information in and out of the reserves, or of news of the AAPA's activities. As Maynard said:

> I must congratulate Mrs McKenzie Hatton on having organised so successfully the branches in these country towns. The difficulties of access and also opposition and intolerance on the part of the provincial towns were quite enough to have disheartened any worker but Mrs. McKenzie-Hatton had gone ahead ignoring all difficulties and had succeeded in firmly establishing the AAPA.[59]

Maynard then described the workings of the central Sydney branch of the AAPA, and announced that the organisation was now a registered body in its own right. This infuriated the Board, which had made every attempt to have the process stopped. The *Voice of the North* crowed '[t]he work of registration had been hurried forward and it was now an accomplished fact that the AAPA was a registered body, with an executive of live-wire men controlling operations'.[60]

The report tabled by AAPA secretary Dick Johnson 'who wears the returned soldier's badge'[61], related that the association had grown rapidly during its short time of operation. McKenzie Hatton had travelled in excess of an exhaustive 5,000 miles promoting the AAPA and informing Aboriginal communities of its existence.[62] Tom Lacey, the treasurer, delivered a financial statement reporting that 'everything was in a healthy condition'.[63] Vice-president I Johnson was also one of the prime motivators in having had the AAPA registered. Johnson's actions were of the greatest importance, and he stressed that 'Now that the AAPA is a registered body the position is assured, and we can go ahead with our progressive policy, which has for its platform many drastic reforms in matters of Aboriginal interest'.[64] The atmosphere was optimistic.

Dick Johnson in uniform. He was the AAPA Secretary in 1925 and a lifelong friend of Fred Maynard.

McKenzie Hatton herself had undertaken an intensive campaign of letter writing; she penned some six hundred letters to the press and other interested groups.[65] Despite the difficulties and opposition that confronted them the meeting highlighted that in all of the districts and towns visited by the AAPA they found support and encouragement for the organisation.[66] Attention was given to prominent members of the public willing to support the AAPA, including the Hon JJ Fitzgerald, Labor member for Oxley.[67] McKenzie Hatton gave vivid descriptions of the widespread support and elation among Aboriginal people that at last some of their own had risen up to oppose the despicable government policy:

> The AAPA was having a wonderful effect on the minds of aboriginals. Despite all the terrible treatment of the past they were an imperious

people, whom persecution and abuse had failed to crush, and the fact that they are now organised into an association has bought a new feeling of self-respect and self-reliance.[68]

Another report of McKenzie Hatton's address at the Surry Hills meeting further illustrates the passionate hope and recognition that had been ignited within Aboriginal people.

> She had been amazed at the aptitude for organisation which the Aboriginal people possessed. Everywhere she went, she was met by deputation's of coloured people asking that branches should be formed. From the remotest parts of the state calls were still coming in asking for a visit from the organising secretary.[69]

The horror of the Aboriginal experience was graphically imprinted upon McKenzie Hatton's mind. She related the terrible distress being suffered and that in all of the locations visited 'deputations came to me imploring me to interview the leaders of Parliament on their behalf'.[70] At one location a woman in deep despair related how she lived 'in daily dread of being moved out of her little house, as the land had been sold to a stranger who had ordered her to be prepared to move at any time. She cried bitter tears as she said. "Oh where can I go? I have lived here all my life".[71]

At another location several married men revealed that they had been threatened by the police and ordered back into the bush:

> They told me that they had been camped on this place all their lives, and now a sale had been arranged and they were told to move away. They were given three weeks to move out back or they would be arrested. The position is becoming more and more acute in regard to the land, and Mrs Hatton said that she had already made an appeal in regard to this matter to the Hon. Mr Loughlin, Minister of Lands.[72]

She went on to reveal that at times the work and travel had been difficult; finances had run out and bad weather had hampered and been 'extraordinarily against her, but people had been kind and had helped her over many a stile and crooked road'.[73] She reiterated the AAPA's stance: 'to see every aboriginal in the country settled on a tiny portion of his own original land, and also that the despoliation of their families as now carried on by Government management be ended'.[74]

The AAPA had unquestionably upped the ante on the level and degree of their protests and directives. The step to now open its own offices in Sydney confounded, alarmed and confronted the New South Wales Aborigines Protection Board. The Board tried everything in its power to block the process:

> Application by Australian Aborigines Progressive Association (Mrs
> E McKenzie Hatton and others) to Register General for registration
> under the Companies Act — Papers to be returned and Department
> informed that the Board is very strongly opposed to the granting of the
> application on account of the unfitness of the promoters who, with the
> exception of Mrs Hatton, are all aborigines, certain available particulars
> re the character of whom are to be furnished; and also because many of
> the objects set forth in the articles of the Association of the proposed
> company are already included among the duties imposed upon the
> Board of the Aborigines Protection Act.[75]

In combating the forces pitted against them Fred Maynard illustrated
that the AAPA would continue to target the mainstream audience with
its grievances. This action was already paying dividends. On 31 July
1925 a non-indigenous organisation calling itself the Australian Natives
Association wrote to New South Wales premier Jack Lang. The ANA
demanded details of Lang's and the government's attitudes towards the
Aboriginal population, and asserted that Aboriginal people 'if properly
treated, invariably make good citizens'.[76] The ANA went on to direct Lang
towards a recent resolution it had passed at its annual general meeting:

> That as the aboriginals should be Australia's greatest asset, the Federal
> Government be requested to immediately appoint Sir John Murray
> as permanent Commissioner to replace all existing authorities, and to
> arrange for the repatriation of the Australian people upon their own
> land on a family basis or in such manner as the Commissioner may in
> his wisdom deem most advisable.[77]

This directive was passed onto the Board; its response was predictable
but nevertheless tinged with apprehension and concern at this previously
unforeseen but widespread agitation against it. Board under-secretary
EJ Harkness responded to the ANA by pointing out that the Board
was entirely comprised of honorary members, bound by the directives
of the minister, who had the authority for the care and protection of
the Aborigines of the state acting upon the *Aborigines Protection Act* of
1909 and its subsequent amendment of 1915.[78] But the Board continued
to receive further demands, a similar one coming from the Australasian
Society of Patriots.[79]

The response to the AAPA's activities was strongest in areas where
widespread loss of land and children was being most savagely experienced.
One area under particular difficulties was the NSW north coast, and so
the town of Kempsey was strategically chosen to be the site of the AAPA's
second conference. This conference witnessed a large Aboriginal gathering
to support the occasion. Newspaper accounts signify the importance and
impact of the Kempsey conference as a:

convention arranged and attended solely by aboriginals. The gathering was unique in the history of the State of Australia; and when the agenda is scanned, one is amazed at the standard reached by these descendants of the original inhabitants. Questions concerning the health and well being of the aboriginal community, of their moral status, their educational improvement, the owning of land in fee simple, and the care and control of their children were amongst the topics discussed, after papers had been read or addresses delivered thereupon. The convention lasted three days, and the whole tone of it was such as it would put many white people to shame.[80]

The conference was a huge success and demonstrated the organisational capacity of the AAPA. Aboriginal people were obviously overjoyed with the organisation and its stance against the Aborigines Protection Board. It must have been such a lift to have had Aboriginal delegates of the organisation moving within the community and conversing with the population on the difficulties they faced as opposed to the Board and its all-white dictatorship and blunt policy of 'we know what's best for the Aborigines'.

The opening function was on 24th December when a party of 200 Aboriginal children were entertained with a Christmas tree. A special Christmas service was held in the church on Christmas evening. On Saturday the 26th the President received the delegates in the Temperance Hall when the business of the conference was commenced and continued up to New Year's Eve. On Saturday visits were made to Nambucca Heads, Coff's Harbour and Bellbrook.

During the session papers dealing with themes affecting our Aborigines were read and discussed. The meetings were largely attended over 700 Aborigines taking part. Our report says: the subjects were relevant, the delegates keen and the visitors included a number of sportsmen from the Northern Rivers and officials of the A.A.P.A. from the city.

The delegates visited the huts of many of the Aborigines, and strong exception was taken to the neglected conditions of the housing of our Aboriginals.[81]

Among the delegates were many notable Aboriginal sporting identities, and there were others of deep spiritual force and power whose presence endorsed the actions of the AAPA in an Aboriginal spiritual context. The conference was also important in demonstrating the support and presence in the AAPA's organisational structure of so many significant Aboriginal families: the Mirandas, the Donovans, the Kellys, the Doyles, the Flanders, the Buggs and many others. Kempsey branch president Eugene Miranda welcomed the delegates:

Miranda requested the greetings and responses of the representatives of the distant AAPA branches. He was widely applauded and was followed on the rostrum by Mr John Donovan representing the Nambucca branch. Donovan declared that the people of the Nambucca region had been the first to answer the call of the AAPA. He had been inspired by his visit to the first Sydney conference, and on his return had rallied his people to the banner and platform of the AAPA. The Nambucca branch was rapidly followed only a week later by another at Bowraville. Donovan indicated that both branches were going from strength to strength and that only recently another was established at Urunga. He declared that his hands were full 'looking after them all'.[82]

During the 1980s Heather Goodall conducted interviews with Olive Mundine, the daughter of John Donovan of Nambucca Heads. Mundine recalled her father as a consistent and vocal opponent of the Board. He had sent 'so many letters to the Board and other authorities that he had built a desk especially for the purpose of writing them'.[83] She described worried gatherings of Aboriginal people at her parents' home. The Whaddy, Buchanan, Doyle and Kelly families were among those who attended and expressed their fears and grievances. They were 'very serious in what they did, they liked to get their facts straight', and they were unanimous and outraged in their condemnation of the Board's actions over the taking of both Aboriginal land and children. 'They were so frustrated, so angry in themselves, that they all got together to decide what they were going to do'.[84] It takes little imagination to comprehend the full impact of the message of Maynard and the AAPA had on groups like this:

> Every area on the mid-north coast gave Maynard and Hatton a warm welcome. Such community support ensured that news of the organisation spread far in advance of the organising visits. By August 1925, eleven AAPA branches had been set up on the north coast, meeting in homes like the Donovans.[85]

Olive Mundine also related to Shirley Maynard, Fred's daughter, 'a message would come through and the people always knew well in advance that Fred Maynard was coming to speak. People would come from all over to hear him talk. The kids got under the shearing shed to hear him talk'.[86]

In conversation with Cheryl Oakenfall, Mundine remembered Fred Maynard and Tom Lacey coming to her parent's home when she was a small child. They spoke passionately of the hardship of Aboriginal people and of the children taken from their families and forced into the indenture system.[87] This rallying of widespread support was inspirational.

> The young men were joining up; they had formed a cricket team and intended to help the fund of the AAPA by holding special matches.

> Mr Shannan, representing Maclean, said the work had a good grip in
> Maclean and they were pushing on the interests of the AAPA there. All
> the responses brought the thrill of a new interest and pulsated with the
> throb of heart to heart talk.[88]

The AAPA was no men-only club; Aboriginal women were very much
a part of the political revolt. During the Kempsey conference a fully
operational AAPA Women's Auxiliary was 'formed wholly of coloured
people'.[89] During the conference this women's group 'performed the task
of seating 3 relays of delegates and representatives and managing the
luncheon in a most creditable manner. In the manner of finances they
were fine; every participant was reminded of the high cost of living by the
Secretary of the Women's Auxilliary with her collection plate in hand'.[90] In
the years ahead, Aboriginal women within the AAPA, particularly south-
coast Koori Jane Duren, were on the frontline of the political fight. This
again draws parallels with Garvey's UNIA, which was revolutionary and
decades ahead of its time regarding the equal place of women:

> In an era when male dominance was almost universal in mixed gender
> organizations whether black or otherwise, women — including Garvey's
> own wife — were unusually prominent in the UNIA movement and
> occupied a number of important positions. The 'women's page' of the
> UNIA paper edited by Garvey's wife Amy Jacques Garvey, spurned
> news of cocktail parties and bridge games, then standard on women's
> pages. It favoured instead articles on such topics as African and Asian
> women liberating themselves from male bondage; articles encouraging
> women to fully develop their individuality; articles extolling women
> as harder workers than men; and articles criticizing black men for not
> working hard enough to provide security for their families.[91]

It is important to note that the overall supportive response generated
by the AAPA during the Kempsey conference was not just confined to
Aboriginal people. Several high-profile local dignitaries attended, and
letters of support and encouragement were received from the Australasian
Society of Patriots and the Australian Natives Association, the latter
relaying 'Greetings, hopes for good results conference ... Aborigines must
be accorded full citizenship rights'.[92]

McKenzie Hatton again delivered an impressive, inspiring report
and address. She was quick to highlight the complete dissatisfaction of
Aboriginal people with the policies and directives of the government and
its agencies. There was, she noted, utter resentment at their treatment
through the government department, which supposedly had their affairs
in hand. McKenzie Hatton again emphasised the importance of the land
issue and the rights of Aboriginal people to it.

The position in regard to the selling of lands, which have always been considered as belonging to the Aboriginal people, was a cause of deep, strong and resentful feeling. She found people huddled on any old corner of the earth, housed in a most wretched fashion. They were asking for a small bit of land upon which to build their homes. This question and that referring to their broken homes, and unsatisfactory method of dealing with their children, were matters absorbing all their thoughts. The AAPA was the one bright spot in the horizon.[93]

Hatton's address received wide applause. Fred Maynard stepped to the rostrum and was given a rousing reception. His paper revealed his activities over the previous months, the registration of the AAPA being one major obstacle overcome. Maynard also praised McKenzie Hatton 'and could only feel that behind that report lay months of self-sacrificing toil'.[94] At the end of his address Maynard delivered the following powerful resolution:

As it is the proud boast of Australia that every person born beneath the Southern Cross is born free, irrespective of origin, race, colour, creed, religion or any other impediment. We the representatives of the original people, in conference assembled, demand that we shall be accorded the same full right and privileges of citizenship as are enjoyed by all other sections of the community.[95]

At the conclusion of the conference a petition to parliament, asking that the AAPA's objectives be granted to the people, was read out and signed. The procession of signatories took till six o'clock to complete.[96]

An overview of the conference appeared in the *Voice of the North:*

The attendance comprised several hundreds of aboriginals from all parts of this State and the whole of the speeches were delivered by representatives of the native race. The various papers were compiled by aboriginals and every motion on the business paper were moved, seconded and supported by coloured speakers.[97]

Although the business activities at hand was the major focus during the course of the conference a strong feature was the fun and entertainment that were also organised to complement proceedings:

A prominent feature of the Conference was an aboriginal Christmas tree which brought joy to more than two hundred little Australian natives. Many donations were received from local residents, storekeepers and Sydney merchants. Mr Albert Woodlands, vice president of Kempsey Branch, impersonated Santa Claus, and possibly the first of his race to fill that role in Australia. During the Conference various musical entertainments were held, the singers and players in every instance being aboriginals.[98]

In the following weeks the resolution and petition were sent to numerous high-ranking officials in the country, including the governor-general and prime minister Stanley Bruce.[99] Sadly, the resolution and the directives sought by the AAPA did not engender the response it richly deserved. The secretary for the Commonwealth Department of Home and Territories noted to the Prime Minister

> As a theory the principle enunciated cannot be challenged but the Australian aboriginal in practical affairs is hardly entitled to be placed on the level suggested by the Association. Aboriginal natives of Australia are not entitled to be enrolled under the Commonwealth Electoral Act, or to vote at Commonwealth elections. The question of whether this disqualification should be continued, or whether it should be removed is one that touches a matter of Government policy. Perhaps this matter might be resubmitted after the elections.[100]

But a newspaper account of the time clearly illustrates that the powers that be were orchestrating a campaign of their own, one to discredit and undermine the Aboriginal political group and its supporters. Chief secretary Mr Lazzarini, commenting on the allegations of Aboriginal ill treatment, reveal a man either totally uninformed or misled on the reality of the situation:

> The statement that the children are torn from their parents is untrue, the parents also being given every opportunity to properly provide for their offspring themselves and having the right of appeal to a court against any action the Board may take. Action is only taken in the cases of gross neglect, and where the interests of the child demand the board's attention. It is extremely regrettable that statements of this nature should be made, as they create an altogether erroneous impression in the public mind.[101]

At a Board meeting held in late 1925, member AW Green was asked to provide a report on Elizabeth McKenzie Hatton. Green was also head of the New South Wales Child Welfare Department, his position on the Board conveniently alleviated any conflict with that department over Aboriginal child removal. The minutes note that 'Mr Green asked to interview the Crown Sol[icitor] with a view to ascertain what action, if any, could be taken against Mrs Hatton'.[102]

***

The year 1925 was a remarkable effort of achievement for the Australian Aboriginal Progressive Association: it became a registered organisation and conducted two large and highly successful conferences in Sydney and Kempsey. It exceeded all its organisers' expectations and experienced phenomenal growth, with eleven branches up and running and over five hundred active members. An optimism was engendered in Aboriginal communities about a better future. The AAPA had skilfully managed to encourage widespread and consistent media coverage of its actions and platform, while placing the New South Wales Aborigines Protection Board in several embarrassing situations. This media coverage was instrumental in informing the wider public of the dire Aboriginal situation for the first time. This message was importantly perceived and directed from an Aboriginal perspective and by Aboriginal leaders.

The confrontation also showed that these Aboriginal people totally contradicted the more widely publicised view of Aboriginal people. They were, much to the surprise of some, educated, articulate and highly informed. The fruits of such knowledge being spread in the wider community were well understood by the Aboriginal leaders who precisely targeted the wider populace. The results and responses of support by such groups as the Australian Natives Association and others who were quick to recognise the Aboriginal message endorsed the success of such a policy.

The AAPA had experienced phenomenal growth, and excitement gripped Aboriginal communities that genuine change was at long last achievable.

6.

A Year of Consolidation

Justice and power must be brought together, so that whatever is just may be powerful and whatever is powerful may be just.

Blaise Pascal

In late 1925 a concerted and well-organised campaign again brought the plight of Aboriginal people back into the public spotlight. Newspaper articles drew attention to two main issues: the practice of stripping Aboriginal people from farmland that they had often worked for decades to improve; and the deterministic government policy of removing Aboriginal children from their families, with its often tragic repercussions. The articles alluded that such a practice had the ultimate purpose of exterminating the Aboriginal race.

> There is the fact, about which there is no controversy, that the children of these aboriginals on the North Coast, on reaching a certain age, are removed from the care of their parents, and the boys and girls sent to different places, and it is further alleged by writers on the subject that their location is withheld from their parents. One of the chief reasons for the diminution of the native races has been the restriction of the birth rate amongst them.[1]

The level of media coverage generated by the AAPA and its membership was having an impact on public opinion. The issue of Aboriginal children being stripped from their parents led to the question being asked in the Legislative Assembly whether it was indeed true that the police had the power to take Aboriginal children from their parents at the age of fourteen. Major HJ Connell asked the House: 'Was the Minister aware that some children had been taken away without their parents consent, thus causing great hardship? And would he inquire into the matter and see what could be done to remedy this state of affairs?'.[2]

One can only speculate at the unease within the inner sanctum of the New South Wales Aborigines Protection Board generated by these public airings of their actions. One thing that must be stated is the Board's refusal to sway under these attacks; this bespeaks its unwavering desire to dominate Aboriginal people at whatever price or cost.

Another article in the *Voice of the North* in December 1925 illustrates the readiness of Aboriginal leaders to take their message on the road and out into the streets to generate support and understanding in the wider community of their issues and case. In an editorial, JJ Moloney commented:

> The most important happening in the way of matters Australian since my last letter was the visit of the aboriginal orators to Newcastle. Messrs. Maynard, Lacey and Ridgeway addressed a large meeting in Hunter Street, Newcastle and received an excellent reception.[3]

In his address at this meeting Fred Maynard was vociferous in his attacks on the Board, demanding the complete overthrow of the current deficient Aboriginal administration policy, and demanding that a Royal Commission be called to 'clear up the present arrangements and install a new system'.[4] Displaying his awareness of the national Aboriginal situation, he highlighted developments in South Australia where Aboriginal farms were prospering, as they had in New South Wales:

> Mr Maynard's contention is that New South Wales should follow the example set in South Australia and place the natives on small holdings in their own right and bring them into competition with every other class of agriculturist on a small scale. The system is reported as working successfully and should be given a trial here. The farm scheme is the most likely one to encourage the family circle, as employment would be found for the juveniles in the primary industries which would equip them for future service and insure their value as citizens of the State.[5]

The Aboriginal political leaders were pressing their people's case for a Royal Commission into Aboriginal affairs and it is obvious that at least some sections of the public, media and even government were beginning to heed the call. Major Connell, cited above for his question to the Legislative Assembly into the automatic removal of Aboriginal children at the age of fourteen, continued to take 'a very lively interest in the welfare of the remnant of the original owners of the soil which still exists in this State':

> Now that the question has attained that measure of public importance which it so richly deserves, we may with confidence anticipate the granting of the Royal Commission, and henceforth the lot of the

coloured people should more nearly approach the protestations of the various sections of the community and some reparation will have been made for the treatment of past years. The incidence of Federal laws will in all likelihood be changed in the near future in a direction which will remove the present discrimination consequent upon the fact of aboriginal descent, which is a foul blot on the fair name of our fair country and should not remain on our statutes a moment longer than necessary.[6]

A further report highlighted the Aboriginal leaders' visit to Newcastle. These leaders were reported as firmly stating that the Board, and the Acts it imposed, had 'outlived its usefulness' and needed to be replaced by a different model. They were firm in the viewpoint that Aboriginal people were well able to take care of themselves and did not need to be regarded as helpless children, as so-called 'wards of the state'. They also reiterated the glaringly obvious warning that the Board's 'objectionable practice of segregating the sexes as soon as they reach a certain age should be abolished for if it is persisted in it will mean the rapid *extinction* of the few remaining aboriginals'.[7]

The Aboriginal leaders were graphically aware of the dire situation that confronted them. Again and again they used the word 'extinction' in describing the end result of the Board's policy and directive. At the conclusion of the Kempsey conference it was decided that Grafton would hold the next AAPA conference, designated for late 1926.[8] Hopes were directed that in the intervening twelve months:

> Changes might take place ... and the pathway very considerably brightened for that valiant band of natives which has survived the callousness, carelessness and even cruelty of the invaders, and who now claim equality of citizenship based on merit in so far as industry and ability to manage their own affairs is concerned. The claims of the aboriginals to have their own homes in fee simple and the right to control their own family life is incontrovertible and must be granted at the earliest possible moment. Nothing less will satisfy them nor that vast section of the community which is in sympathy with their hopes and aspirations.[9]

The Aboriginal leadership of the AAPA was attracting glowing press coverage. Fred Maynard was described as 'an orator of outstanding ability, and in the not far distant future will loom large in the politics of this country'[10], while Lacey was similarly recognised as 'an impressive speaker'.[11] He asserted that, given the opportunity, Aboriginal people were capable of gaining the same position 'as the coloured people of the United States of America, who have their own colleges and universities'.[12]

In an attempt to allay this media barrage and defuse public condemnation of its actions the Board presented its report for 1925 to the New South Wales parliament. Newspaper coverage supported the Board's biased appraisal, painting a picture far removed from reality. The *Newcastle Herald* stated that 'It is the future of the half-caste race that presents a problem', and went on to make comparisons with other countries under British rule: 'In India, despite every effort, the half-caste remains as an unassimilable section of the community. It has to be remembered that the Indian half-caste is for the most part a higher type than the Australian'.[13] In the best of British imperialist ignorance the article went on to assert:

> Many of the half-caste women of *Hindustan have exhibited talent of an advanced order* to which they add *a certain personal charm*, which is not always noticeable in other half-caste races. In Australia, the half-castes are the product of an aboriginal mother, wholly untutored, and but little removed from barbaric races.[14]

The sexist and derogatory appraisal of Hindu women was compounded with its sickening denigration of Aboriginal women. The passage above suggests that Hindu women were desirable sexual objects for the pleasure of British males working in India. This contrast in worldviews is contexualised in the battle between the AAPA and the Aborigines Protection Board. While Maynard and Lacey looked to the United States for models of Black advancement through their own universities and colleges, the Board looked to the so-called superiority of British imperialism. The article soberly concluded that on 'the whole the State is discharging its duties with kindly consideration'.[15]

JJ Moloney continued to stir the pot of agitation through his newspaper editorials. Obviously driven to distraction through the Board's own counterattacks, and its failure to listen to representations made about its activities from several sources, Moloney again reported on the resolutions as adopted by the Australian Natives Association at its recent annual conference in Sydney. These resolutions fully supported Aboriginal people and the issues and grievances they wished to present to the highest levels of government. Moloney reiterated the demand for a Royal Commission, believing that taking evidence under oath would be the only way 'to obtain from those able to speak with authority the facts concerning the conditions and treatment of these unfortunate people'; he also believed that 'the outcome of the Commissions' inquiry should be not merely amelioration of the aboriginals lot but the placing of them upon a proper footing as citizens of this State'.[16]

***

In May 1926 an article in the *Voice of the North* proposed a 'Model Aboriginal State'. A petition to parliament was proposed, putting forth the statement that it was a moral obligation of 'those who came to people Australia that the original occupants should be cared for'.[17] While the petition's proposal reinforced many of the stereotypes and misinformed thought of the day (such as the belief that the Aboriginal race was dying out), section two disclosed an agenda that was in total conflict with the current situation. Indeed, it articulated that much of the government policy, 'although well meaning in concept' had failed because policies were put forward with little thought of their impact or consequences. Recognition was given to the oppression and cruelty directed against the Aboriginal population, of which the government did little to halt.[18] Opinion directed that in a traditional state Aborigines were nomadic hunters and gatherers who were suffering because of the impact of white occupation of their traditional lands. Pastoral spread had depleted and prevented access to their traditional food sources. It argued against the commonly held belief that Aboriginal people belonged to the Stone Age and went on to decree that if Aboriginal people were already recognised as spiritual equals, recognition was also required of their rights. Genuine progress could be accomplished by a decision not to 'treat them merely as chattels'.[19] It was directed that:

> If we return to them areas of country on which they may work out their own salvation safeguarded from the envious eyes of encroaching white population, we shall at least have the satisfaction of knowing that even at the eleventh hour we have endeavoured to redeem any neglect, indifference or maladministration in the past, and to do substantial justice.[20]

At the forefront of the proposal was an Adelaide gentleman, Colonel J Chas Genders — an impressive individual and high-standing member of the Adelaide community. Genders was an accountant, chairman of the United Farmers Association, secretary of the Aborigines Protection League of South Australia, and editor of the Adelaide newspaper *Daylight*. Along with Moloney's *Voice of the North*, *Daylight* was the most pro-Aboriginal newspaper in the country. Until 1925 Genders had been an active member of the Aborigines' Friends' Association (the AFA). He fell out with the promoters of that organisation, breaking away 'through the unwillingness of its membership to consider his own far-reaching proposals for Aboriginal welfare',[21] and formed his own group, the Aborigines Protection League. Genders was the chief architect of the Model Aboriginal State and was on the committee advocating and preparing the petition for the proposal.

The move to establish the state was confronted by widespread opposition and a campaign of misinformation about the proposal. The AFA, Genders' former association, was particularly scathing and made frequent comments in the press that the proposal favoured moving all Aboriginal people to some remote location. The AFA's secretary, the Rev. JH Sexton, was particularly malicious in his efforts to undermine and belittle his former colleague. In an unofficial letter to the secretary of the Home and Territories Department his contempt could hardly be disguised:

> The promoter of the scheme is an unpractical dreamer, and I cannot conceive of the scheme receiving any serious attention from politicians. He brought his dream before the Aborigines' Friends' Association, but he could make no headway with us and resigned, for which we were devoutly thankful.[22]

The proposal gained some international coverage, but again Genders was forced to respond to misleading articles. Famed anthropologist Sir Baldwin Spencer joined the list of attackers with an article in the London *Sunday Observer*. Genders, in his frustration, remained highly diplomatic and respectful in his response, pointing out that some 'who have rushed into print have admitted that they have not read the petition which is being signed for presentation to the Federal Parliament or the manifesto which accompanies it', and that 'the few criticisms we have noticed were not against our proposals, but against what people imagined they are'.[23]

Marcus Garvey covered the issue in the *Negro World*, stating that the authorities in Australia had failed to provide adequately for Aboriginal people and their efforts had been 'fitful and indefinite, while the attitudes of the politicians had been one of absolute indifference'.[24] There is little surprise in Garvey's interest in the proposal as it matched his own idea of a sovereign Black state in Africa.

Quite clearly the movement for an Aboriginal state had much in common with the AAPA's platform and argument about Aboriginal people controlling their own affairs and self-determination. The Model Aboriginal State 'endorsed the idea of self-determination for Aborigines, which was not envisioned by white adherents of protectionism.[25]

Despite the fact that the movement for the Model Aboriginal State was radical and far thinking, Genders' petition still remained ingrained with noble and righteous white directive. It asserted that 'We shall assuredly find that we have races of people who will be of immense help in developing our empty Northern Estate, particularly in the more torrid zones', and that 'we shall find that, relieved of so much attention to material affairs, the self-sacrificing spiritual work of missionaries will be greatly accelerated.[26]

Statements such as these provided the ammunition for opponents of the proposal, who quickly instigated a propaganda campaign to undermine the project and instil in the wider community the notion that the whole process was about moving almost the entire Aboriginal population to some constructed Aboriginal state far from the view and thoughts of the white population. Similar efforts had been made in other areas of the globe, including in the United States with the Cherokee and Apache being moved en masse from their traditional homelands to less favourable under-populated territories.[27]

The proposal had in fact been in the news for over a year. The Adelaide *Register*, on 1 April 1925, ran with the banner 'Proposed Aboriginal State', describing plans to implement a proposal for an Aboriginal state in Arnhem Land.[28] The journalist reported that a public meeting had been called to discuss the proposal, but went on to denigrate the concept that Aboriginal people might be capable of managing their own affairs.

> Here and there a man had been found who might be called an Aboriginal patriot ... They are good men, but he would be a foolish person who would trust any one of them with powers, privileges and responsibilities equal to those of the mayoralty of our smallest borough. The race still lacks its Booker T Washington.[29]

The author, like many of his day, could not conceive of well-educated, articulate Aboriginal leaders like Fred Maynard or Tom Lacey, though it must be said that Maynard and Lacey themselves would never have supported the proposed Aboriginal state. The AAPA's fight was not for a separate and segregated Aboriginal state but for the provision of enough land for each and every Aboriginal family in Australia in their own right and country.

During the debate over the Model Aboriginal State a letter writer in the Adelaide *Advertiser* unwittingly endorsed the AAPA platform:

> I have lived among the blacks for many years and I find that all of them are longing for some little place in their own country that they can call their own; some little place where they are at liberty to carry out their ancient codes unrestricted by the presence of the white man and his stock.[30]

Another writer, Professor Darnley Naylor, also described exactly the platform and stance adopted by the AAPA in NSW at the time. Speaking about the proposed state he said:

> What is needed is a movement of 'uplift', by which the aboriginals will be given their chance, instead of being left exposed to conditions which are certain in the long run to prove no less destructive than

were the swift and more brutal methods of extermination adopted in Tasmania.[31]

Opposition to the proposed state continued. The *Register* reported a meeting of the AFA resolving that 'the scheme being advocated is both fantastic and impracticable and makes no real contribution to the aboriginal problem'.[32] The overall antagonism towards the proposal displays how the opportunity to genuinely improve Aboriginal conditions would continually be marred through the in-fighting, bickering and petty jealousies among the humanitarian, Christian and government authorities who all imagined themselves as the ones best placed to rule the Aboriginal question. The proposal to establish an Aboriginal state held the media's fascination for the next eighteen months. But what does need to be recognised is that, in spite of the confusion and Genders' complete opposition to the idea, there were some who genuinely supported the concept of complete removal and relocation of Aboriginal people, and that it was seriously considered as an option and as a grand solution.

Writing in the *Voice of the North*, JJ Moloney drew the attention of his readers to the concept of the proposed Model Aboriginal State. It is apparent that Moloney was, at this point in time, tentatively supportive of the proposal. He declared 'Is such an experiment not worth trying? Do we not owe some such effort on our part to the natives?'[33]

While the newspapers in New South Wales had maintained coverage of the AAPA's fight to protect Aboriginal land and prevent children being stripped from their parents, knowledge that the organisation was making a far-reaching impact in other states across the Commonwealth had not been acknowledged till now. On 27 September 1926 Elizabeth McKenzie Hatton received correspondence from Genders, who sent McKenzie Hatton an article from the Adelaide *Advertiser* strongly advocating the proposed Aboriginal state. In his letter Genders related that the letters and reports McKenzie Hatton had furnished him with would be published in his newspaper *Daylight*. This reveals that the actions of the AAPA were known to influential people in other areas of the country, people who were both interested in Aboriginal affairs and committed to the task of attempting to improve the Aboriginal situation.

McKenzie Hatton replied to Genders with information about the AAPA. Her letter, and an accompanying article, was printed in the *Daylight* on 30 September 1926. McKenzie Hatton used the article to draw attention to the despicable actions of the New South Wales government in its treatment of Aboriginal people and the subsequent rise of the AAPA:

> Not one word of exaggeration could be possible in recounting some of the stories of oppression, cruelty and insult to them, which I could give. I came over with the idea of joining one of the existing missions

AAPA stalwart Elizabeth McKenzie Hatton at her desk, c. 1916.

at work amongst them, but after serving for some months in the capacity of a missionary amongst the aborigines I came into possession of facts regarding the legislation of New South Wales in the affairs of the aborigines which seemed to need readjustment and in response to a direct appeal from the more enlightened of these people, we formed the Australian Aboriginal Progressive Association.[34]

McKenzie Hatton carefully made the point that the AAPA was an all-Aboriginal organisation made up of men and women possessed of intelligence, resolve and determination to further the Aboriginal cause. She went on to describe how the organisation had experienced rapid growth and had exceeded all hopes and dreams. Importantly, she related that the AAPA was 'the people's own movement and things are done from the viewpoint of the aboriginal which is a vital starting point when beginning to help them'.[35]

McKenzie Hatton was a Christian humanitarian, albeit one undergoing a major shift of understanding. The correspondence to Genders, a noted humanitarian campaigner of the period, is noteworthy in that it clearly illustrates this shift. McKenzie Hatton had earlier written to the secretary of the Aborigines Protection League on the subject of the Model Aboriginal State, and had requested information from Genders on the petition — indicating her willingness to distribute it and present it as a topic of discussion at the forthcoming AAPA conference in Grafton.[36] This indicates that, at the time, she had not discussed the issue with the Aboriginal leadership in any great detail, as they vehemently oppose the proposal at the Grafton conference and in the press.[37] It is also worth noting that when the petition was finally submitted to the Federal House of Representatives in October 1927 McKenzie Hatton's signature was not among the 7,113 who supported the proposal[38]; it seems that by this stage she was more influenced in her political mindset by the Aboriginal leaders than by fellow white Christian humanitarians.

Another article printed in the *Daylight* on 30 October 1926 drew attention to the AAPA, this time to the branch at Nambucca on the north coast of New South Wales. The short article offers a rare glimpse of the AAPA's personnel at a local level, with listed members including Jim Doyle (president), John Donovan (superintendent of the Nambucca Bowraville district), Fred Buchanan (vice-president), Lambert Whaddy (secretary), John Flanders (local secretary, Bowraville), Percy Harvey (Urunga) and Tom Brown (Eungai).

The revelation that Jim Doyle had joined the political fight shows that no Aboriginal person of achievement was safe from the Aborigines Protection Board. In 1922 the notorious Chief Inspector of Aborigines, R Donaldson, had delivered hypocritical praise upon Doyle and his family, describing him as 'a well-to-do man owning several properties and having investments in war bonds running into four figures'.[39] But only four years later Doyle's hard-earned wealth and position was, like all other Aboriginal people, under threat, and he turned to the AAPA to fight for justice as his only means of defence. The fire ignited in Jim Doyle's belly through the actions of the Board continued to burn for many years, and erupted decades later in that of his great-grandson, Gary Foley.

Another member named in the article, Johnny Donovan, was a prominent and well-respected community and sporting identity. It was stated that 'no cricket or football team is complete without his captaincy'.[40] His position and standing in the wider community exemplified in his trusted position as manager of the local timber mill, where it was revealed that he had worked for over twenty-eight years. The article stated that 'It was through his organising ability that Nambucca was first to join up with the Association and he has been all along well to the fore in enthusiasm and interest'.[41]

McKenzie Hatton firmly stated her wholehearted support for the AAPA, and described the constant dread and fear that Aboriginal people in the area were forced to bear in regard to their children's threat of removal. All the Aboriginal office bearers were committed to the cause, despite the constant threat to their own families' wellbeing: 'only their constant vigilance has enabled them to keep their families intact'.[42]

McKenzie Hatton was scathing in her appraisal of the invaders in a highly perceptive analysis of the Australian historical landscape. It is somewhat depressing that some contemporary analysts do not possess the same insight and compassion for the horror of the Australian Aboriginal experience. Many today still fail to consider the ramifications of years of persecution and neglect of Aboriginal people by successive governments:

> The position of the remnant of the original owners of this land … is a blot on State and Church alike. The fact that certain aborigines are camped under petrol tins and without certain knowledge of where their next meal is to come from is a reflection on our boastful civilization.
>
> We may claim that we are not responsible for the actions of the original British invaders who violated their homes, shot, poisoned, burned and mutilated the natives; but we cannot claim immunity from the conditions existing at the present time, and what should not be tolerated for one moment longer than it will take to rectify matters.[43]

What is particularly striking in the letter, only a small part of which is quoted above, is the wrath and condemnation that McKenzie Hatton directs at Church, government and the wider community. Her understanding of the Aboriginal situation is truly amazing, and modern in concept. She realised over seven decades ago the importance of giving control of Aboriginal issues to Aboriginal people and taking heed of their perspectives from their point of view. But this and later letters also dispel the misconception that McKenzie Hatton was herself a member of the AAPA.

The idea that there was white directive within the AAPA structure stems largely from a misunderstanding over McKenzie Hatton's role and involvement. McKenzie Hatton deserves the highest accolades as a tireless campaigner and supporter of Aboriginal people and the AAPA. However, contemporary studies have attributed far too much credence to the assumption that McKenzie Hatton must have been the driving force behind the AAPA. Clearly much of this misconception has been derived from reading archival material — many of the newspaper accounts of the time overstated McKenzie Hatton's role, erroneously implying a white directive. Much journalism of the day was heavily tainted with social Darwinism and therefore suffered in its appraisal and understanding of Aboriginal people and issues. Any concept that there could be highly educated Aboriginal men and women capable of directing their own political and social agenda was out of the realms of the general thinking of the day.

In fact Elizabeth McKenzie Hatton was never a member, let alone the secretary, of the AAPA. She was, rather, a committed and dedicated promoter of the association. There is no better authority or source to clarify this point than McKenzie Hatton herself. In a letter written in 1926, McKenzie Hatton informed Moloney that the Aboriginal community at Tweed Heads was intimidated by the local Christian minister, and consequently no one would step forward to take office with the AAPA. However, a white man who lived with the Aboriginal community had taken up the seal. She related to Moloney:

> Well now, firstly I must attend your request for a personal opinion of Vel — & I must begin by saying he is not an <u>Abo</u>. I found him on Ukerabah Island when I visited the people there & as he put it himself he was 'living on the generosity of the people there, a good many of them working women who had regular days of cleaning at Tweed Heads — we elected officers all aboriginals, but they were scared by Mr Ogilvie a missionary in the vicinity'.[44]

McKenzie Hatton explained that Vel had apparently stepped forward to take up the seal but Vel, she went on to say, was described by the community as an awful liar who had promised all sorts of things. She said 'I wrote at once and told him he could *not* hold office as the AAPA could not allow any to hold any position but Aboriginals'.[45] This statement, combined with the earlier letter to Genders, clearly resolves any misunderstanding over the thought that the AAPA was not an *all*-Aboriginal organisation. In fact, three Aboriginal men held the position of secretary during the AAPA's period of operation: Dick Johnson (1925–26), Sid Ridgeway (1927) and Ben Roundtree (1928).[46]

In the light of this analysis it comes as no surprise to find McKenzie Hatton as the lone white supporter privy to the inner sanctum of the AAPA, expressing international black ideals. Back in 1925 she was reported to have said 'This association is for uplift, *spiritually and socially*. It is progressive in policy. We feel that your best interests have not been considered. The government has no policy for your *industrial* development'.[47] The similarities to Garvey's words are unmistakable. Yet it is inconceivable that she had not been enlightened, encouraged, and directed on the subject matter by the well-informed Aboriginal leaders like Fred Maynard and Tom Lacey. Her ideas flowed from them rather than the other way.

In an interesting development McKenzie Hatton was now under investigation by the Commonwealth Investigation Bureau. This was not the first time McKenzie Hatton had been investigated. The Rehoboth girls' home had been placed under police surveillance at the request of the Board, which had also enlisted a Crown solicitor to seek advice on what action could be taken against Hatton and the Aboriginal political leadership, and additionally sought information on Hatton's activities in Victoria from the Victorian Aborigines Protection Board.

While the new investigation appears to be unrelated to the earlier matters, dealing as it does with a matter from the War Service Homes Commission, one cannot shake the feeling that the Board may have been behind an investigation into Hatton's financial standing. The Board had a history of initiating investigations on the financial dealings and background of people that refused to be silenced. In 1930 the Board clashed with a Mr and Mrs Watson who took the part of an Aboriginal girl in their employ challenging the Board over her trust monies. The Board minutes clearly reveal the devious nature of their practices in securing a 'confidential police report' on the Watsons' 'business character and financial standing'.[48]

***

On 22 December 1926 the Grafton *Daily Examiner* alerted its readership to the imminent Australian Aboriginal Progressive Association conference to be held in their town. The article drew attention to the arrival of Aboriginal delegates and their supporters to Grafton:

> The aboriginal people have at last awakened to the fact that unless they organise they are a lost people. For over a hundred years these people have been close to a civilized people and they have slowly evolved under the poor conditions offered to them, but they have evolved not withstanding the fact that nothing of a definite policy for their development has so far come to light. Missionary effort has had its successful day, and we find the result of these devoted self-sacrificing people everywhere, but under the present legislation the missionaries everywhere admit that their efforts have been limited in regard to anything more than the most primitive teaching. The aboriginal people have caught the progressive spirit of the day and are asking for better conditions and opportunity. The aims of the association are for the development of spiritual, industrial and social interests. The two special objects of the association are first that a small piece of land be given in his own right to every aboriginal to build his home and second

that their family life should be free from molestation. An appeal will be made to the citizens of this town to help.[49]

A week later the *Examiner* followed up with an extensive coverage of the Grafton conference, held at Fisher Park on Boxing Day. The article pointed out that the organisation was on a sound financial footing, and that 'No salaries were paid out of the funds the work being a labour of love, and for the visit part the officers of the association paid their own travelling expenses'.[50]

Several resolutions were carried by those members in attendance at the Grafton conference. These were primarily the same as that first expressed in 1925:

1. That a small portion of land be given in their own right to the aborigines of this country.
2. That the homes of aborigines be free from molestation from the officers of the aboriginal board.
3. That the large sum of money at present in the hands of the [Aborigines Protection Board] be spent in the development of homes and farms for aboriginal people.[51]

As with the Kempsey conference, the social importance of the occasion was not missed by the Aboriginal people in attendance:

An open-air meeting ... was well attended and the coloured artists who provided the musical items received a great ovation ... A concert was given in the Oddfellows Hall at night and once again the platform was occupied solely by aboriginal performers and speakers ... Musical items were presented by Mr L. Kelly (violin) and the members of the gum leaf band.[52]

Significantly, the *Examiner's* article included an informal interview with Fred Maynard. This 'chat with the president' provides an interesting portrayal of Maynard as it highlights his fierce determination and his clear understanding of the issues and battles ahead for Aboriginal people. At first the reporter seems a little taken aback that Maynard, and his colleague Lacey, are intelligent and articulate individuals, remarking that 'both speak excellent English and with logical minds'.[53] The reporter went on to quote Maynard who explained that:

the aim and object of the society was the improvement of the conditions of the Australian aborigines politically, industrially, socially, and otherwise. It was also their desire to enlist the sympathy and support of the public in urging the Government to repeal the Aborigines Act as it existed on the Statute Book today.[54]

Maynard went on to berate the *Aborigines Protection Act*, which he said had not demonstrated any signs of improving Aboriginal conditions since its inception. Further, he declared, despite its obvious failings it had not undergone any improving amendment to rectify the situation. The AAPA he said:

> considered that the Act had seen its days of usefulness, and there was urgent need for a big improvement in the conditions as they applied to the aborigines as a race, and especially their children. He pointed out that the aborigines were in possession of the franchise, but were not given any encouragement to improve themselves or to understand what the franchise really meant for them.
>
> The conditions as they applied to the children of the aborigines were sadly neglected, and the system of educating and segregating the children was causing the spirit of prejudice to manifest itself. There appeared to be no possible help for their development after the primary education. The association claimed, he said, that given equal opportunities they would be able to hold their own in the athletic world and in industrial and political life.
>
> In this connection he instanced his friend Mr Lacey, who had been a prominent first-class cricketer, and Mr C Noble, who was recently ordained a minister of the Church of England. Wherever favourable opportunity had been given for development, he said, the aborigines had proved themselves capable of any advancement.[55]

At the close of the conference it was decided by the delegates that Lismore would hold the next conference in 1927. A vote of thanks to the mayor and the citizens of Grafton and the press was carried unanimously'.[56] In the course of the conference, and acutely aware of national developments and opportunities as they presented themselves, the AAPA and its membership instructed McKenzie Hatton to pen a letter on their behalf to the governor-general in relation to the imminent visit to Australia of their Royal Highnesses the Duke and Duchess of York. Indicative of the importance of cultural identity the AAPA correspondence indicated their willingness to provide the royal couple with an 'old time native display'.[57] The offer stated:

> We have in our membership a number of old full bloods who have kept a sort of corroboree group and are experts at displays of this kind with their paint and war weapons.[58]

A similar event hosted by these Aboriginal performers, held at Kempsey Park in aid of the Macleay District Hospital, raised £34/1/-. The event attracted 'one of the largest crowds seen at the Kempsey Park for some considerable time past', a night-time affair lit 'by motorists who kindly drew their cars up to the ring and kept the headlights going':

> A more fantastic scene could hardly be imagined and it could be readily seen that the old art of wonderful patterns done in red and yellow and white clays, has been by no means forgotten. They then lined up with the leader a few paces to the front and to the accompaniment of a weird chant, which had for its accompaniment the slow and steady beat of two hollow sticks, which gave out a clear cut rat-tat, they began the corroboree. They swayed this way and that, each movement being followed by a peculiar hissing sound.[59]

Sadly, the AAPA's offer to conduct a similar performance for the royal visitors was declined. The Aborigines Protection Board was now on guard against any event the AAPA may use to instigate public support for the Aboriginal cause. There is little doubt that the AAPA members would have made the most of an opportunity to make a public statement to the royals of the dire conditions of Aboriginal people in New South Wales had they been given the opportunity.

The year 1926 was another year of great achievement for the Aboriginal political movement. The AAPA had consolidated its support base within its own community and gained widespread national media coverage. After another year of success the year ahead held promise for justice and recognition of much needed change of policy for Aboriginal Australians.

7.
1927: The Struggle for Liberty

Give us a hand, stand by your own Native Aboriginal Officers and
fight for liberty and freedom for yourself and children.

Fred Maynard, 1927

For the Australian Aboriginal Progressive Association the year of 1927
stands out as the busiest of years. It witnessed great achievements, but also
experienced heartache, mounting obstacles, and deliberate obstruction
to its work. Another highly successful conference was conducted, and
its support base within Aboriginal communities continued to grow and
flourish. Evidence shows that the AAPA had established an intricate and
highly effective network among Aboriginal communities which, despite
the Aborigines Protection Board's attempts at blocking, continued to
provide the AAPA with information on what was happening on the
reserves.

The success the AAPA generated is reflected by the reactions of the
Board, which was now intent on destroying the AAPA and collapsing its
membership. The level of intensity the Board applied to silencing and
breaking down the AAPA stands as testament to the AAPA's success and
vitality. Fred Maynard became a central focus of the Board's attacks as it
attempted to destabilise the support and momentum that the AAPA had
generated.

***

In early January 1927, as was now his custom, JJ Moloney continued with
his coverage and support of the AAPA platform. In his newspaper the
Voice of the North he highlighted the success of the Grafton conference,
and optimistically stated 'The time cannot be far distant when full justice
will be done to the original owners of this land'.[1]

In total contrast the *Newcastle Morning Herald* ran a brutally racist assessment of the Aboriginal situation in an article it ran in March 1927. The *Herald's* article demonstrated the scale of the prejudice and racist attitude of the wider population. It savagely illustrated the great difficulty of the AAPA struggle but showed that for the first time a detailed census had been conducted on the Aboriginal population:

> As a result of the investigation, it was found that the number of aborigines did not exceed 60,000. It is obvious however, that the figures can be regarded only as an estimate, because there are great difficulties in the way of taking a census of nomadic people. At the same time a count was made of the half-castes and these are estimated at 15,000. They can of course, play no part in the preservation of the race.[2]

The accuracy of these figures was questionable, but the writer went on to claim that if the Aboriginal population disappeared it would 'leave but little trace behind them':

> For many years there have been agencies at work to preserve these interesting people. Earnest men and women have moved among them, and have made every endeavour to keep them from the dangers which befall them through contact with white men. But it seems to be all to no purpose. The aborigines except in very rare instances cannot thrive in contact with civilisation. It is impossible to impart into them the qualities which make men responsible citizens and at the touch of civilisation they develop physical defects, the result of which are only too evident on any of the reserves which are maintained for their protection.[3]

The journalist was clearly confident in his assumption that Aboriginal people were headed for oblivion, and in comments that may have been directed at the *Herald's* rival Newcastle newspaper the *Voice of the North*, he went on to say:

> The fact may be regrettable, and there are many well meaning people who are unsparing in their denunciation of the treatment of the aborigines since the commencement of settlement. But their affection for the race cannot alter the characteristics of the race and these make it impossible for the aborigines to continue to exist in the settled portions of the Commonwealth.[4]

It was left to Dorothy Moloney, JJ Moloney's daughter, and partner in the *Voice of the North* to respond in print and direct readers back to the realities of the situation. In a letter printed on 11 April 1927 she criticised 'The same old story of callousness towards the mothers of aboriginal children. Again the absolute negation of our professed Christianity', and expressed hope that the Colonial Secretary 'Mr Lazzarini has grasped the facts he will take such steps as will remove the cause of all these complaints'.[5]

However, perhaps in the interests of balance, the same issue of the *Voice of the North* featured a letter to the editor from JS Needham, chairman of the Australian Board of Missions. Needham defended the role of the Church, and mission work in general, in relation to Aboriginal people. 'We do what Miss Moloney says should be done, and put the welfare of the aboriginals as the first charge on our funds', said Needham.[6]

Needham was blind to the fact that the Church was complicit in continuing to treat Aboriginal people as children within strictly confined and controlled institutions, thereby keeping them helplessly bound in the Church's tentacles:

John J Moloney, editor of the Newcastle newspaper, Voice of the North. *He was a staunch AAPA supporter.*

> We consider that the most effectual way of helping the aboriginals is by a policy of reserves where they can be segregated and under religious influence. This we have learned from long experience. Senator Pearce, when Minister of Homes and Territories said that the work of raising the natives could best be done by the Churches with financial aid from the Governments and all decent people.[7]

The archives reveal that the resolutions laid down by the AAPA and its membership at its conference in Grafton were rattling those in the halls of the establishment, and were even making an impact at the premier's department. The Board was forced to reply to correspondence received through the state premier and the Colonial Secretary Brutnell over allegations received from McKenzie Hatton regarding the treatment of Aboriginal people.[8]

Directives such as this, along with relentless pressure from the likes of the Moloneys, unsettled the Board. Perhaps through their newspaper the Moloneys were hoping to inspire the support of the wider community and its sympathy when they stated that 'we are pleased to see that the general public are at last awakening to the importance of the aboriginal question, both from humanitarian point of view and the economic point of view'.[9] JJ Moloney drew attention to the rise of the AAPA and its startling progress in such a short space of time, saying 'This body has been in existence but a few years, yet it has done yeoman service in placing the case of the aboriginals in its proper light before the Governments and the people of Australia'.[10] Moloney reinforced the AAPA's manifesto for land, citizenship and the right to protect their children from being taken from them. It was clearly stated that the future of Aboriginal affairs and issues must be controlled and directed by Aboriginal people themselves.

The same issue of the *Voice of the North* provides further proof that the AAPA's fight was having a national impact. A letter from Richard Tomalin, the manager of Mount Leonard Cattle Station at Windorah in Queensland, Tomalin wrote to the AAPA stating:

> The drastic and utterly unlawful method of taking away their female children would not stand if taken direct to a British Tribunal, as under the law the freedom of a British subject cannot be taken from him, and I consider a father just as much justified in using all means he chooses to defend his children from being forcibly removed from their parental care, more so even than a banker in defending his gold.[11]

Tomalin was glowing in his estimation of the many Aboriginal people he had came into contact with, and his knowledge of the needs of Aboriginal people was quite clear: they needed and deserved their own land. Tomalin explicitly stated that to improve Aboriginal conditions, government control had to stop, and each Aboriginal group deserved a 'piece of land in their own district'.[12]

Tomalin's complete lack of trust in any government — state or federal — was hammered home as he advised that all hope rested in going above and beyond governments for justice:

> Direct action should be taken by proceeding straight to the Throne through his excellency the Governor-General, stating their rights as British subjects have been taken from them and their wrongs placed before him. This is a special matter and is not an interference in the methods adopted by the British Colonial Office, is not interfering with the colonists in the management of their own affairs, it is a different subject altogether. I hope therefore, that your Progressive Association will have success and quickly.[13]

Tomalin was unaware that, through the AAPA, one Jane Duren had already informed the palace of the Aboriginal people's plight, only to see the Crown to pass the buck back to the state government in Australia — even though these were the very same perpetrators of most of the wrongs committed against the Aboriginal population.

On the 14 June 1926, Duren — an Aboriginal woman from Moruya on the south coast of New South Wales — had written to King George V. Duren aligned herself with the AAPA platform in fighting to protect Aboriginal land. Much has been written about William Cooper's letter from the late 1930s, which was also directed at the king. But while Cooper's letter was never sent, Duren's was posted and is stamped by the Private Secretary's Office at Buckingham Palace on 27 July 1926.

Duren's impassioned plea highlighted the plight of Aboriginal children of Bateman's Bay being forced from the local school. 'I beg to state that it is months and months since those children were at school and it is a shame to see them going about without education'.[14] As Duren pointed out the school was a public school and, if this was the case, why were Aboriginal children denied their place in this 'public' institution? Duren noted that education was compulsory under state legislation, but this was obviously only the case if you were white. She related how the Batemans Bay community had been prolific in its attempts to draw attention to their children's plight, describing how they had been 'writing to different places, namely, the Minister of Education, the Child Welfare Department, the Aborigines Protection Board also to our Members of Parliament but cannot get fair play'.[15] Duren concluded by revealing that the Aboriginal reserve land itself was under threat to white appropriation:

> Even the reserve land where the coloured race were bred and born the white race are trying to have them turned off on to another piece of

land. It is unfair and I hope you will see that fair play be given let them stay on the land that was granted to them.[16]

Duren did not receive a reply to her letter, though archival evidence reveals that the governor-general received notification of the letter to the king, and he dictated and delegated responsibility back to the New South Wales state government. Nothing was done to improve the lot of the south-coast Aboriginal community.

In the months following Tomalin's plea, the *Voice of the North* continued to report on the actions of the Board. Dorothy Moloney reported how 'very little has been achieved regarding the actual betterment of the coloured people', but did note that 'raids on homes have been less frequent'.[17] Perhaps this was an indication that the AAPA and its supporters had forced the Aborigines Protection Board onto the back foot — if only temporarily — in regard to its rampant assaults on Aboriginal family life.

However, one can only guess at the real impact of the AAPA's actions; certainly Jane Duren's communication to the Crown would have sent a shiver of fear down the backs of these officials, as one thing they did uphold was the ideology of the empire and the Crown. Now they were fully alerted, though, and while they still carried out their objective of dismantling Aboriginal culture and wiping away all trace of Aboriginal people, this was now carried out in a more covert manner. Part of this new tack was to focus on the destruction of the AAPA and its membership.

Dorothy Moloney revealed the tragic plight of one Aboriginal family, the Milligans of the Hawkesbury River, and in that revelation took another swipe at governments and Church alike. The Milligan family consisted of Eva Milligan, her four children, an aged grandfather and a disabled uncle. Their only regular income was a war pension, amounting to thirteen shillings and sixpence per fortnight. Moloney reported:

> The little hut is quite unfit for such a family to live in. It is neither rain nor wind proof. The wind whistles through it and that the children have not died of pneumonia or other similar diseases is remarkable evidence of the hardihood of the Australian people. Furniture, utensils, or ordinary comforts are conspicuously absent and the surroundings, taken as a whole, are complete evidence of the callousness of the Government regarding the welfare of the remnant of the original owners of this country.[18]

Moloney presented Eva Milligan as an example of enforced hardship and opportunity denied, a key plank of the AAPA platform.

The AAPA issued, an appeal aimed squarely at the wider population on the plight of the Aboriginal community, in the same issue of the *Voice of the North* that Moloney's description of the Milligans appeared, and it requested that the appeal 'appear in all the metropolitan and country newspapers'.[19] This appeal to the private sector was coordinated with a petition and appeal to the New South Wales Premier, Jack Lang. The basis for the petition was the series of resolutions handed down at the Grafton conference.

The petition reinforced the strong Aboriginal push for land. The opening expressed the need for the government to recognise a 'reasonable repatriation in our own land'[20] and that the Aboriginal populace of New South Wales were worthy of the 'full privileges of citizenship', which were long overdue. Fred Maynard addressed his letter to the editors of several newspapers and directed his appeal to the men and women of New South Wales. It was cleverly couched in the Australian notions of fair play and equality for all.

Maynard stated that the plight of Aboriginal people is 'A National subject, and that we are not asking for anything in Kind or Money,' and that 'Our only request is the rights of citizenship for ourselves and our families'. He went on to articulate the just nature of the Aboriginal demands:

> Our requests are few and their equity cannot be denied. We confidently anticipate your kindly endorsement of this just request, feeling sure that it is your desire to give our people and their children every reasonable opportunity in our own land. We are only asking to be given the same privileges regarding our family life as are being freely offered to people from other countries.

Committing our plea for assistance to your characteristic love of fair play.[21]

The full extent of the demand covered the entire spectrum of Aboriginal complaint encompassing the social, political and economic:

A. That all capable aboriginals shall be given in fee simple sufficient good land to maintain a family.

B. That the family life of the aboriginal people shall be held sacred and free from invasion and that the children shall be left in the control of their parents.

C. That the incapables of the Aboriginal community (the direct liability of the Government consequent upon neglect in the past) be properly cared for in suitable homes on reserves, the full expense of such establishments to be borne by the Government.

D. That the supervision of all such aboriginal Homes, Hostels or Reserves be entrusted to the educated aboriginals possessing the requisite ability of such management.

> E. That the control of aboriginal affairs, apart from common law rights, shall be vested in a board of management comprised of capable educated aboriginals under a chairman to be appointed by the Government.[22]

The petition, addressed to Jack Lang, concluded by informing the premier that this response was from a 'united people' intent on justice and demanded that the government 'Restore to us that share of our country of which we should never have been deprived, likewise those family rights which are the basis of community life'.[23]

On 11 July 1927 Dorothy Moloney was once more on the attack in her column, drawing attention to newspaper reports highlighting horrific details of Aboriginal men being forced to work in chain gangs in Western Australia.[24] Further disturbing comments were voiced by a church minister in Adelaide where he 'openly stated that he had flogged the natives in the Northern Territory'.[25] Building on what she described as a remarkable response from concerned people over the condition of the Milligan family, Moloney used these reports in her article to focus the forthcoming state election. As she pointed out:

> The position of the aboriginals in New South Wales now transcends all other political issues and at the coming elections it will be of such supreme importance that every candidate for political honours will be called upon to defend his attitude in regard to the appeal of the aborigines for proper repatriation and full rights of citizenship.[26]

In her article, Moloney revealed that all Aboriginal people in New South Wales possessed the right to vote in the state election, and this caused a ripple of discomfort in political circles. It was a fact that was little known to many, including Aboriginal people themselves:

> The aboriginals are ... under no disability whatsoever and are as much entitled to a vote as any member of the Civil Service. The position is different in Federal political circles. The founders of the Commonwealth Parliament had not the vision of Wentworth, and they excluded the native population from the franchise. The Royal Commission which will sit in the near future to make suggestions regarding the amendment of the Constitution will be asked to reverse this unfortunate flaw, since it is our boast that the people of this country have a say in making the laws which they are expected to obey.[27]

Reference in the article to the imminent Royal Commission was gaining momentum. Only weeks earlier, state premier Lang had been informed by prime minister Bruce that 'a deputation which recently waited upon my colleague, the Minister for Home and Territories, requested that an

"Extra-Parliamentary" Royal Commission be appointed to enquire into the present status and general conditions of the aborigines'.[28]

Bruce's directive clearly illustrates that the campaign led by the AAPA and its supporters over the previous two years was having an impact. When premier Lang consulted the Board, he received predictable advice from the Under Secretary. Having 'considered the question', the Board was of the opinion that:

> ... the control and care of the aborigines in this State has been as successful as circumstances would admit, and, having in view the time and trouble involved, the Board doubts that the appointment of a Commission to inquire into the matter is called for, so far as New South Wales is concerned.[29]

Jim Fletcher interviewed former Board secretary AC Pettitt several decades after this decision was made, and raised the issue of the Board's decision and defensive viewpoint regarding the call for a Royal Commission.

Fletcher: [Elkin] tends to think that all the changes that occurred in the 30s were the result of his pushing. Now I'm not so sure.

Pettitt: Well I don't know what he was doing behind the scenes as it were but there is probably a lot of truth in that.

Fletcher: He seems to have been very active that's for sure.

Pettitt: Oh yes, and there's no question about it, the change *was* overdue.

Fletcher: That's odd you know because in the late twenties the Prime Minister wrote to the Premier of New South Wales and suggested the appointment of a Royal Commission and the letter was passed on to the Board and I can remember the Board writing back to the Premier and saying 'We don't think there is any need for a Royal Commission. We think that the methods that we've adopted and the course we've taken and the result we've got are as good as can be expected'.

Pettitt: When was that?

Fletcher: It would have been in 1927 and in about eight or nine years, the Board's attitude seems to have completely changed.[30]

Pettitt made no reference or recognition to the fact that this was Aboriginal-led agitation and that the Board itself was the significant reason for stopping their progress. However, the pressure was beginning to build on those in positions of prominence, the prime minister's department continued to receive correspondence calling for a royal commission, and the coverage in the media of Aboriginal political agitation continued to gain support. A report in the *Northern Star* alerted the public of the AAPA's petition to the premier and revealed that Fred Maynard and Tom Lacey were "'the moving spirits" of the organization'.[31] The article revealed that 'one of the main complaints is that the girls are taken forcibly from reserves and placed in service at very small remuneration'.[32] Further disclosures regarding these forced removals reveal the frightening reality of Aboriginal life. The AAPA disclosed that the Board's actions and policies, including the apprenticeship, system suggested 'a quiet working scheme looked like an attempt to *exterminate* the race'.[33] An AAPA member revealed that at Lismore recently:

> one mother hid her children in the bush so that the board's inspector could not take them, while all the aborigines in another reserve left in a body when three girls were taken forcibly and placed in service … Another member said that New South Wales on the face of it appeared to offer the aborigines a blanket and rations for what was in reality his country in the first place.[34]

A news article in the *Voice of the North* related the movements of Elizabeth McKenzie Hatton who had been in Queensland and was expected back in New South Wales in the not too distant future. The article stated that it had been through the actions of McKenzie Hatton and the AAPA that patriotic societies had rallied their support to the Aboriginal cause, and that that response had been instrumental in making significant alterations to the oppressive actions of the Aborigines Protection Board. Dorothy Moloney acknowledged McKenzie Hatton for providing evidence of the cruelty Aboriginal people in Western Australia had been subjected to, namely, a photograph of men linked in heavy constraining chains. Moloney expressed that she herself had doubted the press reports of such activities as being out of the realms of all possibility. But she pointed out:

> the camera cannot lie; and now Australia must be ranked with the Congo and Soudan in its treatment of human beings. I was also under the impression that there were Christians in Western Australia, but possibly I am wrong again; yet I cannot remember a single utterance by any Christian regarding this barbarous treatment of the real owners of this country. I never dreamed that the Southern Cross, which floated on the Peninsula of Gallipoli, would wave over conditions as delineated in that gruesome picture.[35]

Moloney proposed that such terrible actions had been kept well from the view of the recently visiting Duchess of York, who would not have tolerated such blatant abuse of any human being's most basic of rights. Her article went onto reveal other callous acts, such as the treatment of seventy-year-old Andrew Barber of Windsor, NSW. Barber was refused the aged pension on the grounds that he was not a 'full blood'. But as Moloney went on to point out:

> In the Civil Service this man would be retired at 65 years of age with full superannuation rights, but because Mr Barber has borne the heat and burden of the day in the open fields of his native land he is turned away in his old days and seemingly, he may fish and hunt for a living so far as the pension authorities are concerned. The matter will I presume be brought under notice of Mr Bruce and he may induce Dr Page to spare a few pounds from his surplus millions for the relief of this aged Australian who in the sunset of life is excluded by the reason of the colour of his skin.[36]

In spite of constant revelations in the press, the powers that be were marshalling their forces against the AAPA and its allies. Archival sources reveal the level of both the Board's ignorance and its firm commitment that it would, despite evidence to the contrary, block all avenues of Aboriginal progress and quash the flame of Aboriginal hope which the AAPA offered. Correspondence from the Board to the NSW premier reviewing the AAPA's petition provides graphic detail of its total opposition and firm belief that it, the Board, had Aboriginal welfare matters well in hand. The Board indicated to the premier that it had considered the AAPA's proposals in depth at its last board meeting and had arrived at conclusions that are openly hostile and racist in its tone. In response to the AAPA's demand for enough land for each and every Aboriginal family in the country 'the Board, knowing the nature of the Aboriginal, is of the opinion that in most cases the property would be quickly disposed of for more liquid assets'.[37] The response was ignorant of the facts and biased only on opinion. It emphasised that there was nothing stopping 'industrious Aborigines from purchasing their own blocks of ground and establishing their own homes thereon'.[38] Further insult was delivered when the report indicated that 'Aborigines have a decided advantage over a white man in poor circumstances, inasmuch as the former is provided with free housing, rations, blankets, clothing and medical attention'.[39] This picture of a tranquil Shangri-la was far removed from the tragic and savage reality of the Aboriginal experience. It remains today as it was in the 1920s: extremely difficult, if not impossible, for Aboriginal people to achieve equal employment opportunities and an economic base from which to conduct themselves. Contravening and twisting the facts, the Board declared in relation to the accusation of forced child removal that:

> The family life of the Aboriginal population is at the present time held sacred and free from invasion, unless the Board has very excellent reasons for interfering in the interests of the children, with a view to

ensuring that they are not exposed to immoral and contaminating influences.[40]

The AAPA's call for full responsibility and accountability of the government in dealing fairly with the Aboriginal 'incapables' who were suffering as a direct consequence of past and present neglect was, from the Board's position, totally unfounded: 'The incapables of the Aboriginal community are at present receiving care and attention at Government expense at the Board' Reserves and Stations'[41]

The Board dismissed the AAPA's call for Aboriginal people to be placed in charge of their own affairs, describing this as 'impracticable'.[42] This report of the Board's marks a turning point in its actions, from despised toleration to outright hostility towards the AAPA. The hatred and intent of the Board to target the AAPA and its membership for 'special' treatment cannot be disguised.

***

On 23 August 1927 Fred Maynard received a letter from the NSW premier, Jack Lang, responding to the AAPA's petition. One can only speculate on the disgust that Maynard must have felt upon reading Lang's letter, with its thinly disguised rebuke of the AAPA and Aboriginal people in general. It did not take Maynard long to respond in kind, and his contempt and disgust bubbled over in his reply to the premier. Maynard's letter remains to this day as one of the most powerful, inspirational and insightful ever penned by an Aboriginal activist. Maynard indicated in his opening paragraph that the AAPA's members were firmly under the impression that Lang had obviously never sighted their original communication: '[We] are of opinion that you have not had an opportunity to peruse the document in question as [we] feel sure you would not have passed same as being the calibre of correspondence befitting a statesman'.[43] Maynard redirected Lang to look once more at their demands, as it was beyond the comprehension or understanding of the Aborigines Protection Board author: 'He appears to be perfectly satisfied with the inference of inferiority and the despicable innuendo which pervades his remarks concerning the Australian people'.[44] Maynard's message was powerful, articulate and extremely modern in its approach:

> I wish to make it perfectly clear, on behalf of our people, that we accept no condition of inferiority as compared with the European people. Two distinct civilisations are represented by the respective races. On one hand we have the civilisation of necessity and on the other the civilisation co-incident with a bounteous supply of all the requirements of the human race. That the European people by the arts of war destroyed our more ancient civilisation is freely admitted,

and that by their vices and diseases our people have been decimated is also patent, but neither of these facts are evidence of superiority. Quite the contrary is the case ... The members of [the AAPA] have also noted the strenuous efforts of the Trade Union leaders to attain the conditions which existed in our country at the time of invasion by Europeans — the men only worked when necessary — we called no man "Master" and we had no king.[45]

Many current-day analysts have described the early Aboriginal activists as conformist and pressing for an equality based on the ability of Aboriginal people to adopt a European and 'civilised' means of living. While it is true Fred Maynard did emphasise to Lang that 'Our people have ... accepted the modern system of government which has taken the place of our prehistoric methods and have conformed to same reasonably well',[46] but none of this is evidence that Maynard or the other members of the AAPA did so with any thought of abandoning or denouncing either Aboriginal culture or a distinct Aboriginal identity. In fact, the evidence points to the contrary.

What must be remembered is the target audience to whom the Aboriginal leaders were writing. When they wrote to the authorities they strategically constructed their writing and petitions. As evidence throughout my book demonstrates, the AAPA platform was very much grounded in a cultural context. The full message of Maynard's letter to the premier was confrontational and cutting in its delivery. He targeted the sinister activities of the Aborigines Protection Board and highlighted the full impact of historical reality since 1788, including invasion and the subsequent one-sided war that was waged against the Aboriginal population. Maynard hammered home the point of Aboriginal rights to land: 'The request made by this Association for sufficient land for each eligible family is justly based. The Australian people are the original owners of the land and have a prior right over all other people in this respect.'[47]

Maynard directed the majority of his venom at the Board and its leadership. He could not contain his disgust or displeasure at their complete failure to understand the issues and to try and sweep them under the carpet:

The remark in the Chief Secretary's letter concerning the opportunities for the Australian people to purchase suitable land is refuted by recent proceedings in the Lands Department when the age-old homes of the native people were sold over their heads. The further sneer that they are given blankets and rations is refuted by the refusal of the Government to grant a Royal Commission to inquire into the conditions under which the native people live in this state. The recent exposure of refusals of

> Old Age Pensions to our elderly people and the statements that these
> old folks were not receiving any sustenance from the Government have
> not evidently been observed by your Chief Secretary, in view of what
> he writes regarding help bestowed.[48]

Maynard did not hold back his scorn for the Board's response that it held
Aboriginal family life to be sacred, that Aboriginal children were not
under assault except in 'extreme circumstances', or that the 'incapable'
Aboriginal people were not in such a state as a direct result of government
policy. The outright rejection by the Board of the AAPA's response to allow
Aboriginal people themselves to control Aboriginal affairs was addressed,
and Maynard put it to Lang that:

> [Y]our personal interest in this movement for the complete
> emancipation of our people [is sought], and in any inquiry you may
> inaugurate you are assured of the fullest support of the members of
> the [AAPA] and the leaders of the people at the various places where
> aboriginals are located.[49]

In the course of the correspondence between Maynard and the premier
there was a change in state government, and premier, in New South
Wales. The Board through EB Harkness, wasted no time in providing
new premier, Thomas Bavin, with a distasteful and biased appraisal of
both the Aboriginal situation and Maynard's correspondence:

> From personal knowledge of the writer [Maynard], combined with a
> recognition of the difficulties inseparable from the aborigine question,
> I have no hesitation in recording the view that the representations of
> Mr Maynard, who is not altogether a disinterested party, should not be
> allowed to unduly occupy the Premier's time.[50]

The Board would in every way possible block Maynard and attempt to
discredit both him and the other AAPA leaders. The correspondence went
on to describe Manyard as 'a full-blooded black (either American or South
African) whose voluble manner and illogical views are more likely to
disturb the Australian aborigines than achieve for them improvement of
conditions'.[51] The insinuation and the insult was quite distinct: Maynard
was too intelligent to be Aboriginal, and he had to be dismissed as a
troublemaking Black from some other overseas location. The Board was
probably aware of Maynard's ties to the Coloured Progressive Association
and the Universal Negro Improvement Association, and drew on that to
undermine and denounce the Aboriginal leader.

Dorothy Moloney kept herself informed of these developments. She
penned another cutting editorial which highlighted that the AAPA had
no intention of backing away, but would in fact up the ante in its level of
their protest. Moloney revealed to her readers:

You will be delighted to learn that the Australian Aboriginal Progressive Association has decided upon militant action in order to attain the objects for which it was formed. The leaders of the movement are all educated men and they have realised that by meekly accepting a policy of inferred inferiority the position of their people has become worse instead of better. They are therefore rejecting such an inference, and claiming equality with all other branches of the human family resident in Australia. The hour is always supposed to produce the men, and in this instance there has been no disappointment.[52]

Moloney was glowing in her recognition of Maynard, describing him as a 'polished orator', but even more so of Tom Lacey:

From end to end of N.S.W the name of Lacey is known and admired. He is a keen debater and will be hailed as a modern Moses. The slogan 'No more slavery in N.S.W' will reverberate throughout the length and breadth of continent, and will not only have the effect of breaking the chains off the aboriginals in the prison gangs of West Australia, but will straighten out every grievance which the native people are enduring under the respective Australian Governments in general but those of New South Wales particularly [53].

The article pointed out that Aboriginal people had been receiving promises since the arrival of the First Fleet, but that 'the promises have not materialised'. In spite of the Board and the premier's response to the AAPA's petition Moloney's tone was positive and forward looking: 'the prospects have changed, and the policy of the A.A.P.A will in all probability preserve its entity for many hundreds of years to come'.[54]

***

On 14 October 1927 Fred Maynard penned a letter to a young Aboriginal girl. Little did Maynard realise how this letter would intensify the Aborigines Protection Board's hostility towards him.

Maynard's letter was as a result of communication received at the AAPA offices in Crown Street, Sydney. One thing the association had established and could rely on was a very effective Aboriginal community network, one that kept them well advised of developments within their widespread communities. In this instance the AAPA received notification that a young Aboriginal girl removed from her family had been placed into the apprenticeship scheme. Maynard's correspondence indicates that this girl, aged only fourteen years, had been raped at her place of employment and — when found to be pregnant — was put on a train at the Board's directive and sent to Sydney. There she had her baby, which apparently died at birth. Incredibly and callously, the Board put her back on a train and sent her back to the very place where these assaults had been committed. When news reached Maynard he reacted immediately. His compassion and anger at the sickening tale are self-evident.

His heart-rending letter begins with an opening of comfort, 'my darling little sister, I am speaking to you now as a big bro'.[55] His heart was 'filled with regret and disgust' as the girl was 'taken down by those who were supposed to be your guide through life':

> What a wicked conception, what a fallacy, under the so called pretence and administration re the Board, governmental control, etc I say deliberately, the whole damnable thing has got to stop and by God[s] help it shall.[56]

Maynard was incensed that the law condoned the attacks against Aboriginal girls and allowed the perpetrators to escape without penalty, but also stated that he would pursue the man responsible. Further, he assured her that:

> I may tell you and, listen, girlie, your case is one in dozens with our girls, more is the pity, God forbid, those white robbers of our women's virtues, seem to do just as they like with down right impunity and mind you, my dear girl, the law stands for it. There is no clause in our own Aboriginal Act which stands for principles for our girls, that is to say any of these white fellows can take our girls down and laugh to scorn yet? with impunity that which they have been responsible for they escape all their obligations every time.[57]

He asked the girl for particulars relating to the assaults and the identity of the man responsible. It is obvious that Maynard hoped to use the case to damage the government's policy as well as the perpetrators of the crime. It has been theorised that it was the questions over paternity and the attacks against the Board itself in Maynard's letter that, later, the Board hoped to use to damage the Aboriginal leader's reputation.[58]

Sadly, however, Maynard's letter never reached its destination. The manager of the station opened the letter and, on reading its contents and noting the AAPA logo, sent it directly to the Board saying that 'when I saw the heading on the paper I glanced through it I then considered it my duty "to send it on to you to let you see what is doing"'.[59] The Board tried to use Maynard's letter to discredit and defame his reputation.[60] Hindsight shows that they failed miserably in their objective, and instead of diminishing Maynard's reputation they only enhanced it in the face of his heartfelt anguish for this young girl's plight.

One important aspect of Maynard's letter is the difference in its construction compared to those sent to white politicians, bureaucrats and organisations. In total contrast to the letter to premier Lang, the construction and thrust of the message is entirely different when delivered to an Aboriginal recipient. Maynard was scathing when he warned that sinister motives lay behind the Board's policy and intentions. 'Make no mistake. No doubt, they are trying to exterminate the Noble and Ancient race of sunny Australia'.[61] His contempt toward the Board and Act could not be contained: 'What a horrible conception of so called legislation, Re any civilised laws, I say deliberately stinks of the Belgian Congo'.[62] He also stated that the Board's intentions were hiding behind 'these so called civilised methods of rule, under Christianised ideals, as they claim of civilising our people under the pretence of love'.[63] Maynard felt the whole process had to be confronted:

> [T]hese tyrannous methods, under the so-called administrative laws re the Aboriginal Act, have got to be blotted out as they are an insult to intelligent, right thinking people. We are not going to be insulted any longer than it will take to wipe it off the Statute Books. That's what our Association stands for: liberty, freedom and the right to function in our own interest.[64]

He drove it home that Aboriginal people had been pushed too far:

> Are we going to stand for these things any longer? Certainly not! Away with the damnable insulting methods which are degrading. Give us a hand, stand by your own native Aboriginal officers and fight for liberty and freedom.[65]

A background motif to the rising hostility between Maynard and the Board was the national debate over the proposed Model Aboriginal State, and the granting of land to Aboriginal families in general. Academics from overseas offered their opinion on systems established among the Maori of New Zealand and the Navajo of the United States, and debate inevitably raged over the ability of Aboriginal people to manage their own affairs. Dorothy Moloney used her *Voice of the North* editorials to reinforce hopes that the debate in Canberra over the model state would generate genuine recognition and radical changes to Aboriginal policy, but pointed out that the majority of the debate in federal parliament was directed to the northern regions of Australia. She revealed that the conditions in the settled east were no less important for affirmative action. The conditions of Aboriginal people living in New South Wales were very different to conditions in the northern areas of the continent. A great number of Aboriginal people living in New South Wales had some degree of education and many had gained experience working in industries such as farm and station work, timber-getting and the fishing industry. What was needed was an opportunity and a 'fair go'.

Would the recent change in state government in New South Wales change the political landscape? Previous coverage in the *Voice of the North* emphasised that the AAPA had tried every means of diplomacy in trying to instigate government intervention and change to Aboriginal policy. Having grown disenchanted through lack of response, the Aboriginal leadership had threatened that it would, from this point, on take more militant action. Fred Maynard had indicated that he and the other leaders of the AAPA were well aware of the franchise available to Aboriginal people to vote in the state elections, and it was now time to play that card.

Evidence from an article in the *Voice of the North* indicates that the AAPA had indeed taken steps to inform Aboriginal communities of their voting rights, and had convinced Aboriginal people that voting was important and could pay dividends. Moloney highlighted that the AAPA's 'effective propaganda during the recent elections', which 'made fully apparent the voting power of the coloured people ... more especially in those electorates where the figures at the booths were very close for several candidates'.[66]

The article indicates that the AAPA's influence had made an impact in the election. But the AAPA's elation at the time over its triumph in mobilising Aboriginal voting is tempered by our current knowledge of the repercussions that surely resulted from such action and perceived interference. There is little doubt that the militant directive of the AAPA of that time would have been viewed with great distaste and would have been indicative of revolt in the eyes of some narrow-minded whites. These events undoubtedly further generated anger and concerted hostilities being directed at the Aboriginal leadership and the AAPA.

However, the AAPA was not to be diverted from its aims. A newspaper report stated that the AAPA was about to meet Bishop D'Arcy Irvine of St Andrew's Cathedral, Sydney, to discuss 'many matters appertaining to the regulations governing aboriginals in this State, and I am positive that their appeal will be met in the most sympathetic manner'.[67]

The AAPA had dared to venture into the heartland of Sydney Anglicanism!

The AAPA's push for equality continued to gather momentum and to garner press interest. An article in the Sydney *Evening News* alerted the public about an Aboriginal organisation which was pushing for claims of equal rights with whites. The article revealed that:

> In Sydney there has been formed the Australian Aboriginal Progressive Association, which boasts educated leaders and capable speakers. It has for president Mr F W Maynard. Recently the association appealed without success to the Lang Government for certain concessions and the members are now enlisting the aid of church organisations.[68]

The AAPA's policies were becoming better known to the wider public in the cities, and the following day the *Sydney Morning Herald* ran a story that centred on the meeting between the AAPA leadership and high-ranking church officials. If the Church leaders expected a group of acquiescent Aborigines, they were completely wrong. The *Herald* banner declared 'Aborigines — Want Racial Equality — Appeal to Churchmen — Letter To The King'.[69]

> There was a strange mixture of humour and pathos at a meeting at the Chapter House last night between the Bishop Coadjutor of Sydney [D'Arcy Irvine], the chairman of the Australian Board of Missions [the Rev J S Needham] and seven aborigines, members of the Australian Aboriginal Progressive Association. The natives sought the opportunity of stating their claims to racial equality with the whites and certain other concessions for the less-educated brethren.[70]

Importantly, the article illustrated and reinforced that the AAPA was not some male-only organisation, but that Aboriginal women were heavily involved in its leadership and direction:

> Two of the natives were women, and one of them, Mrs Duren, astonished Bishop D'Arcy Irvine by saying she had written to the King.
> 'To the King?' he asked.
> 'Yes,' replied Mrs Duren, 'I addressed it to King George V, England'.
> 'Do you think the King received it?' asked Bishop D'Arcy Irvine.
> 'Well,' replied Mrs Duren, 'I registered it, so he must have'.[71]

The article revealed that Maynard, a 'self-educated aboriginal', acted as spokesman for the group and intelligently pleaded their claims for the repeal of the existing Aborigines Act, and its substitution by another that would be more agreeable to them and would make no distinction between them and the whites.[72]

The leaders at the meeting discussed the subject of the much-publicised push for a Model Aboriginal State. They emphasised the fact that their membership totally rejected any such notion which sought to remove Aboriginal peoples from their traditional lands and remove them en masse to a remote location. It is clear that Aboriginal people believed that the model state idea was in fact a proposal to move all Aborigines by force to the Northern Territory. This opinion was certainly held on the north coast of New South Wales, and the strong opposition of Aboriginal people there was confirmed at an AAPA meeting in Lismore later in November, at which the people stated that 'they preferred to live where their homes were'.[73] The Aboriginal fears were strongly announced to the church leadership by the AAPA representatives:

> Mr Maynard declared defiantly against the proposal to institute a native State in the Northern Territory. Some of the less civilised tribes, he declared, would insist upon adhering to their age-old tribal customs, and the place of their birth.[74]

Maynard stated that any directives aimed at Aboriginal people and issues warranted representation from each state and that, from Maynard's standpoint, would undoubtedly necessitate Aboriginal input, direction and representation. JS Needham, of the Australian Board of Missions, sought to ease the leaders' suspicions when he explained:

> that there was no intention forcibly to remove natives from their usual haunts, but that it was proposed merely to segregate the natives and secure them from molestation. Mr Maynard seemed placated. He insisted however, that the natives should be provided with their own communities, with schools and other public buildings and should be supervised generally by educated and capable aborigines.[75]

Maynard had every reason to be distrustful as, only four years earlier, the very same Needham — in obvious fear of the 'yellow peril' invading and overwhelming the white Australian population — proposed using the Aboriginal population to create a protective zone in the far north of the continent:

> He says that if a line were drawn from Cooktown to Carnarvon they would cut off practically half the continent which, at present, does not have a white population of 6,000. The only way in which that portion could be defended against the yellow heathen hordes and the purity of the Australian race retained was to place the blacks on large reserves in that area under such conditions that they would increase and thus populate it. There were 70,000 Australian blacks still remaining. These could be placed in the northern part of Australia and create a buffer zone.[76]

Needham must have been suffering from amnesia. At the meeting with the AAPA delegates he attempted to discredit the Aboriginal argument that, if given fair opportunity, Aboriginal people were capable of achievements the equal of anyone. He claimed that there had been 'many instances where natives had been given all opportunities to improve themselves, but with two exceptions — that of the well known David Unaipon and a Queensland girl — they had disappointed the white protectors, who had endeavoured to help them'.[77]

One can only hazard a guess at Maynard's contempt at such an ignorant response. Maynard immediately replied that Needham's movements with regard Aboriginal people and communities were vastly different to his own. Maynard's rebuke dictated the injustice and total lack of equal opportunity that confronted Aboriginal people:

> Wherever he had come into contact with his own people he had discovered the most appalling conditions. At Macleay River he had found 60 natives, men, women and children, suffering from starvation. The conditions were most horrible. The public did not learn about it because there was a 'hush' policy. In reply to Bishop D'Arcy Irvine, Mr Maynard said that help from the police was not sought, as it was feared that the children would be taken away from the parents. That was considered crueller than starvation.[78]

Jane Duren slammed home the inequality of Aboriginal existence through education and the inability of the Board to respond to Aboriginal complaint and ill treatment:

> Mrs Duren said she had complained to the Minister for Education of the exclusion of black children from the State school at Batemans Bay. The Aborigines Protection Board was a nice name, she had told officials of that office, but when this kind of thing occurred where did the protection come in? Influence was everything. If one did not have it, one got nowhere.[79]

Maynard concluded his remarks by once more raising the issue of Aboriginal land and complained that 'some of the land set aside in the early days of Australia was gradually being alienated from their use', and also urged that 'the liqueur prohibition clause in the Act should be abolished as it was insulting to the Aborigines'.[80]

Needham responded that he would place their requests before the proper authorities. He revealed to the press that, as a result of the meeting, he would personally take an interest in the claims of the AAPA. His comments were, however, guarded and unsupportive. 'I am not sure the best is being done for the aboriginals,' he stated, but then went on 'Some of their complaints are legitimate, but I am quite certain that a number of their requests cannot be granted'.[81]

Despite their appeal, the AAPA's hopes of widespread support among the religious brethren was not forthcoming. While the Church as a whole was not prepared to join the AAPA in 'an assault on the State Government', it was 'pressing for the appointment by the Federal Government of a Royal Commission Inquiry'.[82]

The outcomes of this important meeting were, in general, mixed for the AAPA. However, one interesting aspect about the report may well be worth raising.

Back in 1996 I had the good fortune to interview the much-respected Dhungutti Aboriginal elder Reuben Kelly in relation to my grandfather.

Reuben grew up at Bellbrook Mission and had vivid memories of my grandfather. In the 1920s, when Reuben was a young lad at Bellbrook, he was one of the boys assigned to sneak off the mission without the authorities knowing in order to take messages and run along the riverbed to meet up with Fred Maynard under a bridge.[83] During this time, Maynard was prevented by the Board from entering Aboriginal missions or reserves as the authorities feared, or at least claimed, that he was instigating revolt.[84] As already mentioned the intricate Aboriginal information network was efficiently attuned. Those on the reserve were uncannily aware when Maynard was in their vicinity. Boys would sneak off with letters and notes for family members in other locations around the state, and also kept Maynard abreast of conditions and treatment of Aboriginal people at these locations. Reuben reminisced of Maynard:

> I remember he used to call me Mr Brunton, in reference to my clothes. My Grandmother had made me a shirt from Brunton flour bags. [Maynard] was the first man to speak out about the atrocities. The poisoning, the murders, the penal system put into our area. He was one of the greatest. You could see it in his eyes … Other people before him were afraid of the government.[85]

Reuben recalled the anti-Aboriginal cultural regime of the mission, re-membering how 'we couldn't keep up our language and our culture': …

> If I spoke to elders — say my grandfather — and they were communicating in the old ways, the manager or pimps would see that the old man was banished up to 25 miles away from the mission. But they would keep his family. He would not be allowed to visit or see them. The whole process was about breaking down the culture. I don't know how we stood it for so long. Anyone who spoke out was cruelly treated and harassed.[86]

But Reuben brought an even more disturbing scenario to light. He was adamant that Maynard was undermined from within his own group. Reuben concluded 'our people are too often bought and seduced by promises and accept the crumbs and carrots dangled before them'.[87]

There may be some evidence in Reuben's remark from in *Sydney Morning Herald* report of the meeting between the AAPA members and the church leaders. When mentioning that for, the most part, the spokesperson for the group was Maynard, it also revealed that some 'associates punctuated his remarks with interjections'.[88] This may be nothing more than overexcitement by some of the AAPA's members rather than encouraged division within the AAPA structure. Certainly, evidence to come will reveal the strength and solidarity of the Aboriginal leadership of the AAPA which, contrary to popular belief, did not cease in 1927.

Indications are strong that the AAPA was progressive and committed to its task with long-range plans of ingenuity in the pipeline. Therefore, one can assume that although it is highly likely that an attempt to cause division within the AAPA ranks was a possibility and may have been attempted, it nevertheless failed.

***

In late November, as the year 1927 drew to a close, an article in the *Northern Star* reported the AAPA's presence in the town of Lismore, where its annual conference was conducted at the Lismore showground. The journalist revealed that 'interesting information concerning the aims of the organisation known as the Australian Aboriginal Progressive Association was supplied at the meeting'.[89] Elizabeth McKenzie Hatton delivered a speech, which outlined the objects and directives of the organisation and the success that it had achieved already. It was revealed that 'practically all the executive officers were full-blooded aborigines' and McKenzie Hatton highlighted 'the remarkable organising ability which the majority of those had shown'.[90] McKenzie Hatton emphasised that 'although the Society had been in existence for only about four years it had already accomplished much good work. Its chief aim was to afford a say in the management of their [Aboriginal] own affairs'.[91] In a cutting and again a far-sighted assessment she revealed that the 'State Government had once put aside thousands of pounds to help the natives, but so much of it had been wasted in expensive administration that very little of it had been expended on the purpose for which it was really intended'.[92]

However, having only partially succeeded in gaining the support of Church leaders in Sydney, the AAPA was finding it similarly difficult to develop alliances at all levels of politics. The AAPA and other groups had invested time in courting the federal minister for Home and Territories, Charles Marr, of the incumbent Nationalist–Country Party coalition government. An article in the *Northern Star* reveals that Marr had taken up Aboriginal issues with gusto, but as a result was attacked and severely rebuked in parliament by the member of the Northern Territory, Harold Nelson, and members of the Labor opposition — including future prime minister James Scullin. The result of these attacks may well have intimidated Marr from further support for the Aboriginal cause.

The article revealed that 'taking Ministers to task is now a popular recreation in the House of Representatives. Mr Marr, Minister for Home and Territories, had his turn just as Mr. Bruce had moved the adjournment of the house'.[93] Marr had been drumming up support for Aboriginal issues in the house, and it is apparent he had no forewarning of the level of hostility such a move could make.

Marr accused Nelson of employing Aboriginal people as 'labour at slave rates' at a mine in which Nelson held interests the Northern Territory.[94] But Nelson responded in kind, repudiating the claims and making counter claims of his own. At one point, Marr said that 'Mr Nelson had called him the "Minister for Black Labour"'[95] over his sympathetic attitude, but Nelson had powerful allies, including Scullin, and the sarcasm and attacks that Marr was subjected too ensured that any hopes the AAPA had in a federal political ally were greatly diminished.

In November 1927 the Grafton *Daily Examiner* reported 'Aborigines Protest — Protection Act A Disgrace — The Colour Line — Children Taboo At Schools'. The story concerned a meeting of the AAPA in Sydney at which Fred Maynard had vented his anger over the flagrant breaches of human rights inflicted upon the Aboriginal community. 'We consider that we, as human beings and the rightful owners of this soil, have a claim upon the rights and privileges that others enjoy,' stated Maynard, and went to assert that the present system of administrating the Aborigines Protection Act was a disgrace to the community. 'A great many of our children,' he added, 'are taboo at the public schools because of the colour line. They are considered to be wanting in intelligence and devoid of reason.'[96]

But by this stage Maynard was under concerted media attack from the Aborigines Protection Board, which continued with its efforts to discredit the Aboriginal leader as he was proving to be a committed adversary and thorn in their side. Reports in two newspapers reveal that Board Colonial Secretary Bruntnell was forced to respond in the Legislative Assembly to questions about reports in newspapers of starving Aboriginal people in the Macleay Valley.[97] The questions were put was in response to allegations made by Fred Maynard in the AAPA meeting with the Church leaders, and reported in the *Sydney Morning Herald*. Bruntnell insinuated that he was now in possession of a police report that contradicted these statements. The police sergeant for the area stated that 'He had been in close touch with the settlement and said the allegations that aborigines had been starved were not substantial'.[98] This statement fails to disprove Maynard's assertion at all.

Dorothy Moloney delivered another powerful editorial in the *Voice of the North*, informing readers of the recent visit to Newcastle of the widely travelled Elizabeth McKenzie Hatton:

> The cruelty of the system in regard to the children of capable aboriginals was stressed as likewise the treatment meted out to them in respect to the selling of their lands and the failure of the authorities to provide for their reparation … Mrs Hatton was most heartily cheered when she

demanded that the system of semi slavery at present in vogue shall be excised from the Statute Book of New South Wales.[99]

Moloney stated that the AAPA and its supporters had undertaken an intense and concerted program of travel and lectures during the year. Fred Maynard had also visited and spoken in Newcastle, where he 'delivered a lengthy address dilating upon the hardship and injustice still being endured by the remnant of his people'.[100] Once again Maynard stressed the point that Aboriginal people were 'competent to take their place on equal terms with the Europeans in the primary industries, and at the same time demands for them the full rights of citizenship'.[101] The audience, by the report, was driven to voice full approval of the Aboriginal leader's demand that every Aboriginal 'in this State should receive in fee simple sufficient good land upon which to maintain a family'.[102] Moloney expressed the view that the pressures exerted by the AAPA and their supporters could be expected to necessitate wide-sweeping change in Aboriginal administration. These reforms would surely be 'granted by the present Colonial Secretary [Bruntnell]' and remove:

all barriers preventing the attainment of the modest demands made by the A.A.P.A in its manifesto recently published, and which was placed in the hands of all aspirants for Parliamentary honours prior to the recent elections. The members of the present Legislative Assembly cannot plead ignorance of existing conditions and by reason of the knowledge now in their possession they will be enabled to give an intelligent vote on this subject when it comes before them for decision in due course. [103]

This was certainly an optimistic outlook as Bruntnell had, as already evidenced, attacked Aboriginal calls of ill treatment, describing the allegations as fabricated and false.

***

The bigotry, hatred and ignorance that was rampant in some sections of the Australian community came to the fore during a heated exchange in the Grafton *Daily Examiner* for three weeks in late 1927. On 7 December the newspaper published the opening salvo from Mr W Ager of 'Trafalgar', who was incensed that the local agricultural show had involved Aboriginal people as a part of the show's performance program, and stated that 'Blacks should be left where they should be — way back in the bush'.[104]

A response was only three days in forthcoming from one Herbert Ramsay, a local member of the Free Presbyterian Church, who sought to apologise to Aboriginal people for such an insidious and sickening attack:

> Sir — I hope that the aborigines of the Clarence River will be wise enough to take no notice of the unjust and uncharitable letter of Mr. W Ager, which appeared in your issue of Wednesday last. I consider it was most uncalled for, un-Christian, and unkind.[105]

Predictably, the exchange developed into one of defence (from Ramsay and several other writers) against attack (from Ager). Of Aboriginal people and their supporters, Ager believed that 'When they come into the towns and intermingle with white civilisation they contract diseases of the whites, forget the moral code of their tribe, imbibe drink, make themselves a nuisance generally, and breed a mongrel race'[106], and ridiculed Ramsay's stance.

This heated exchange was not missed by the AAPA. Elizabeth McKenzie Hatton wrote her own letter, pointing out that she had been directed to respond by the Australian Aboriginal Progressive Association:

> They [the AAPA] are grateful to those who have written in such kindly terms about them, and thank the editor for the generous space given to these letters. In this respect the *Daily Examiner* is keeping apace with the large daily papers of Sydney, for during my recent visit to the city I have found that the aboriginal question is now occupying the attention of the Australian public, and also that our broad-minded politicians. We have at last awakened to our obligations.[107]

McKenzie Hatton enclosed a cutting from one of the major newspapers reporting on comments of praise for Aboriginal people made by American anthropologist Dr Lloyd Warner. Hatton inferred that Warner's comments stood in stark contrast to the ignorance of people like Ager and showed 'a brighter side to the picture than that suggested by your correspondent, whose vulgar and somewhat contradictory remarks have raised this debate'.[108]

On 26 November 1927 an event took place that, on the face of it, had little to do with the future of the AAPA, but which may in fact have been something of a turning point in the fortunes of the association. The marriage of Sid Ridgeway and Cora Robertson at the Baptist Church, Chatswood, marked a short break in political activity for the AAPA leadership. The day was very wet, but a happy one for the newlyweds. At '4:30 pm Miss Cora Robertson was joined in holy matrimony to Mr Sid Ridgeway, youngest son of the late King of Karuah and the Queen who is still living on the Karuah Mission Station'.[109] Mr R Childs of Eastwood, an old friend of the mission, gave the bride away, and Fred Maynard was Sid's best man.

Happy as it was, the marriage may however hint at another chip in the framework of the AAPA's eventual break-up. The Ridgeways were moved to Goulburn, where Sid had gained employment in that district. The loss of the Ridgeways — to both the AAPA and as staunch allies to Fred Maynard — may have played a part in the stalling of the AAPA's momentum. The Ridgeways' marriage, and subsequent arrival of children to some of the high-ranking AAPA officers, also opened up an avenue of fear and intimidation previously not open to the Aborigines Protection Board. They could now threaten and intimidate the AAPA office bearers and their families. The threat to remove children from their families was a very real one and an insidious form of intimidation.

The year, in which so much was achieved, was to end badly for the AAPA. On 29 December a letter was penned to Fred Maynard by the under-secretary for the premier.

> With reference to your recent communication to the Premier respecting various matters in connection with the Aborigines of this State, I am directed to inform you that these questions have now been inquired into, with the result that it is not considered that there is any justification for the Premier interfering with the administration by his colleague the Colonial Secretary of the Aborigines Protection Act and matters arising thereunder. It is felt that the Aborigines Protection Board is dealing sympathetically with a very difficult social question, with due regard to the peculiarity of the position in respect of the aborigines.[110]

The Board had asserted its bureaucratic authority. This response would have dealt a sickening blow to the Aboriginal leaders. The hopes they held of genuine change again thwarted by narrow-minded webs of deceit and control.

8.

The Final Curtain

The Australian Aboriginal Progressive Association had modelled much of its platform and agenda around Marcus Garvey's Universal Negro Improvement Association and, like that movement, the AAPA declined into near total erasure from public memory. Garvey's movement, while today being justly recognised as the biggest Black movement ever assembled in the United States, was all but forgotten only a decade after his enforced departure from that country.

There is now little doubt, both here and in the United State, that the authorities were very much a part of the erasing process. The memory of success achieved and the hope both the UNIA and AAPA instilled in their people was recognised as a dangerous threat in the two societies and was systematically obliterated. There is no shame from an Aboriginal perspective in that acknowledgement; it reflects the power that the government and its agencies have used with great deliberation to silence and break down the resolve of the Aboriginal population in both its actions and also its memories. No less a commentator than Chika Dixon reflected on the 1960s:

> Looking back on the movement, from the time we went on the 1963 Freedom Rides to Moree and Walgett, things have changed tremendously. In those days you could only get two blacks involved — me and Charlie Perkins — with a lot of white students on a bus. Today when you ask blacks to move on a certain issue, you can get a

heap of them. But not then. Even up until '68 when we tried to march 'em down George Street to support the Gurindji you could count the blacks on your fingers, or at the most fifteen or twenty. Now we can muster 600 or more, so the pendulum has swung.[1]

It is important, given that context, to recognise that government policy did have success in obliterating the memory and legacy of Fred Maynard and the AAPA. Even the late Kevin Gilbert said 'There was, however, as late as the Sixties, no Aboriginal movement … The need for something resembling a 'black movement' in an organised sense became more apparent in the Sixties and Seventies'.[2]

I am certain that Gilbert would be happy to be proven wrong on that statement and would be the first to recognise why he was unaware of, and indeed denied knowledge of, the much earlier Aboriginal movement and AAPA struggle of defiance. Evidence reveals that the AAPA carried on into 1928 and beyond with positive and exciting developments already planned in their pursuit of justice for all Aboriginal Australians. Filled with hope, the AAPA had no intimation that its own destruction — both actively and in memory — was imminent.

***

In early 1928 Dorothy Moloney reported in the *Voice of the North* a new initiative on the part of the AAPA — the publication of its own newspaper:

> I have the pleasing intelligence to impart that the Australian Aboriginal Progressive Association is about to launch an official press organ to be known as *The Corroboree*. The word signifies 'a big talk' and as the new paper will have plenty to talk about, we may expect some critical articles concerning the lot of the aboriginal people in this State … Once again the power of the press will be demonstrated, and the cause of the minority pressed home upon the majority.[3]

But only a month later Moloney passed on sad news, news which may ultimately have played a part in curtailing and restricting Elizabeth McKenzie Hatton's motivation and political enthusiasm: McKenzie Hatton's husband, Tom, died suddenly at their home in Queensland.

***

After years of demands for a royal commission into Aboriginal affairs by the Aboriginal political activists and their supporters, a commission on the constitution finally came together in Canberra in early 1928 to discuss concerns in relation to Aboriginal issues. The AAPA and its membership was undoubtedly heartened and hopeful that the commission would put forth far-reaching amendments to the current restrictive and insulting legislation. The Aboriginal leaders, however, would have been dismayed that they had not been asked to provide some input to the commission itself, but nevertheless directed support and advice. The signatures of Elizabeth McKenzie Hatton and Fred Maynard appeared on the AAPA correspondence and the opening was supportive to the commission and hopeful that a genuine outcome would result.

A message to the commissioners reveals the national perspective in the demands of the AAPA. The Aboriginal leadership was adamant that the Commonwealth was better equipped, more capable and accountable of managing Aboriginal affairs than the states. It directed that 'the present system of constituted laws and administration under the six states as now constituted as obsolete'.[4] However, the message became most heated when it discussed the situation in New South Wales and the utter reluctance and stubbornness of the government and Aborigines Protection Board to listen to Aboriginal advice and pleas for assistance: 'We claim that, after many appeals to the New South Wales Government, no attention has been given to these matters — the horrible abuse still continues'.[5]

McKenzie Hatton and Maynard argued that the assault upon Aboriginal girls was particularly sickening. It was common practice for girls of fourteen to be 'torn away from their parents and their homes' and 'put to work in service in an invironment [sic] as near to slavery as it is possible to find'.[6]

The demands put forward by McKenzie Hatton and Maynard again directed attention to the Aboriginal fight for land in their own country. The message went on with a heartfelt plea on behalf of the Aboriginal population, particularly those who had suffered terribly in the wake of greed and thirst for land at the hands of the white population. Maynard cited those Aboriginal men who had worked in the service of government, often as trackers, who received land grants in exchange for 'service rendered' — only to be stripped of the land they had cultivated for decades and see it sold off 'to the highest bidder'[7]

While some Aboriginal people had benefited from their work with the police in earlier days, as in the above example, the same could not be said at the time that Maynard wrote his message:

> The fact that the police are the administrators of the aboriginal protection board in country places is a matter of keen disapproval with the members of the association. Unfortunate men, women and children, the old ones, the weak ones of the community, are insulted bullied when they appeal for [the] help which a generous government has set aside for them and their use; it is quite a common thing TO FIND OLD PEOPLE STARVING RATHER THAN APPEAL TO THE POLICE FOR HELP. [8]

The message strongly stated that the Aboriginal predicament was entirely the fault of the government's so-called protectors, and that the enforced and regimented policy was a thinly guarded attempt to breakdown Aboriginal people and culture, physically and mentally, the ultimate aim being their eventual obliteration.

Three weeks later the results of the commission were revealed to the wider public; the disappointment among Aboriginal people and their supporters must have been overwhelming, as their anger, hostility and frustration was clearly evident. In the *Voice of the North* Dorothy Moloney encouraged people to respond to the commission, pointing out that the commission:

> may be taking evidence in your town, and it is incumbent upon all good Australians to make an effort for the betterment of our dark people. They deserve better treatment and the responsibility devolves upon us to see they get it.[9]

Moloney gave Newcastle, the home of the *Voice of the North*, a glowing endorsement in its stance for Aboriginal rights:

> Our own city of Newcastle has set an example to the whole Common-wealth by reason of the constant agitation maintained during many years by a local organisation for the betterment of the conditions prevailing amongst the aboriginal section of the community.[10]

This is an interesting aside. While not wanting to paint an unrealistic picture of Newcastle as some sort of beacon of anti-racism, prejudice and oppression, its relationship with Aboriginal people does deserve greater scrutiny. Newcastle's place as a blue-collar working class industrial city did undoubtedly play a part in providing greater support and tolerance towards Aboriginal people and issues.

Some years ago, when conducting an interview with respected elder Reuben Kelly, he directed me to consider place and locality in the context of relationships between Aboriginal and non-Aboriginal people. Reuben emphasised that it was indeed strange that some sections of the country were inexplicably more generous, tolerant and understanding towards Aboriginal people, while others were not.[11] He related that Armidale and Kempsey had always been very difficult and racist centres towards Aboriginal people, yet Tamworth and Port Macquarie (both in close proximity) afforded greater compassion and opportunity.[12] Reuben asked a series of pertinent questions: Why was this so? Who were the settlers and people of these areas? What was their background? Were they Scottish, English, Irish, Welsh, European, Asian or whatever? What was their religious and economic position? What secrets remained buried in these locations? All of these issues may well have contributed to the positive and negative actions in some areas.[13]

This has relevance when one tries to understand why Newcastle became such a magnet for Aboriginal people and their families. Unquestionably during the 1920s Newcastle did offer the Aboriginal leaders the opportunity and platform to express their grievances. Fred Maynard received constant newspaper space and spoke in the main street of Newcastle to a large gathering, and on other occasions addressed local nationalist groups and organisations on the rights and fight of Aboriginal Australians.

The onset of the Great Depression may have sown further seeds of understanding especially in Newcastle, with some white residents experiencing firsthand the hardship suffered by the Aboriginal population for years before. During the Depression some twenty-seven camps sprang up in and around the city of Newcastle. Many of those out of work were forced to live in tin humpies or tents with dirt floors, no water, electricity or heating.[14] These non-Aboriginal Novocastrians were forced to comprehend the everyday experience of Aboriginal families, the effect of dislocation, loss of self-esteem and the general 'wondering as to where your next meal was coming from'.[15] Some of these people, for the first time, shared life's experiences with Aboriginal neighbours, people whose suffering predated the Depression and extended well beyond its end.[16] The non-Aboriginal occupiers of these Depression camps left with a far greater compassion and understanding of the plight of Aboriginal people. In many cases it was probably the first time that they had lived in close proximity with Aboriginal families. While the people in the camps had been marginalised from the rest of society they experienced a deep sense of community with both the Black and white fellow campers. These experiences were to make a more permanent mark on the city of Newcastle. Many years later Pastor Frank Roberts, himself a much respected political fighter for Aboriginal rights, spoke in warm tones of the Steel City and revealed that this was the very reason why — in 1974 — it 'was chosen for the great gathering of the tribes' that took place there one weekend.[17] The *Herald* reported that:

> [T]he cause of the Aborigines has struck a sympathetic chord … Their aspirations and objectives are better understood and better supported than in most other Australian communities. Here they are confident of finding the 'atmosphere and climate necessary to press our claims'.[18]

Pastor Roberts was an Aboriginal man of great respect, knowledge and experience after 'fighting the good fight on behalf of his people for 25 years'.[19] He was certainly a man well credentialed to give comment on the worth of Newcastle as a favourable location for Aboriginal people and issues. The industrial working class nature of Newcastle also presented working opportunities for Aboriginal men where, in other parts of the state, there were none. One woman recalled that upon leaving Karuah Mission with her husband and his father they 'decided to take a chance and come to Newcastle and it turned out a good move because he was able to gain employment in the heavy industry'.[20] Another man recalled leaving Purfleet Mission at Taree as a young child; his father was successful in gaining employment at Stewart & Lloyd and worked their for years because 'in Newcastle there was no colour bar...the Black man and white man were equal'.[21] Newcastle historian John Turner has indicated 'clearly, oral tradition is stating that Newcastle was an attractive alternative to mission life because racism was less overt'.[22]

In 1993 Newcastle City Council, at the forefront of the reconciliation process, presented a commitment to Aboriginal people in the Hunter. The commitment was drafted in consultation with the local Aboriginal community and supported Aboriginal people and the wider community 'working together for a treaty or other instrument of reconciliation'.[23] In a symbolic and powerful statement the council acknowledged 'and grieves for the loss by the indigenous peoples of their land, their children, their health and their lives'.[24]

Therefore, the statement by Dorothy Moloney back in 1928 on the worth of Newcastle to stand alongside Aboriginal people and confront oppression was not without substance and possessed a long continuity. The organisation that she praised was of course the local Australasian Society of Patriots. The ASP, to its credit, endorsed the AAPA's platform and incorporated some of the Aboriginal demands in their policy statement, that all Aboriginal people living in a 'primitive' state be placed under the control and care of the federal government and that all Aboriginal people 'should be provided with sufficient good ground, housing, accommodation, implements and live stock for the proper maintenance of his family, with full citizen rights'.[25] The ASP also reflected the Aboriginal political stance on an Aboriginal place in the education system: 'That all aboriginal children or children of aboriginal descent should be allowed free access to the State schools'.[26]

> In spite of her recent bereavement, the *Voice of the North* reported in early April that Elizabeth McKenzie Hatton was shortly expected to 'visit Newcastle and Sydney in the near future ... to establish the new newspaper, which is to be published under the auspices of the Australian Aboriginal Progressive Association'.[27]

Ongoing discussions in the *Voice* about the proposal for a Model Aboriginal State indicate the national focus that Aboriginal agitation had generated. Miss D Roper from South Australia, a writer to the *Voice* on the subject, had worked at Point Pearce in South Australia, and it is likely that the influence of the AAPA inspired their South Australian counterparts to political mobilisation.

The coverage given by the South Australian newspaper, the *Daylight,* to the AAPA and their activities in New South Wales signify an undoubted catalyst for igniting similar demands and action in that state. One Aboriginal writer from Point Pearce praised the efforts of the Aborigines Protection League (a white South Australian organisation) in condemning 'compulsory segregation as unrighteous. It would undoubtedly be a very unkind policy in this enlightened Twentieth Century'.[28] The Aboriginal author attacked the South Australian government's inability to consult with Aboriginal people themselves 'and endeavor to arrive at a good understanding regarding what should be done'.[29] The writer called for the granting of agricultural land on which Aboriginal people could sustain themselves. In a striking similarity to the New South Wales land revocation, he noted that the Poonindie Mission station near Port Lincoln was 'cut up and taken away from us'.[30] A month later further correspondence from Narrunga Johnny, also of Point Pearce, was printed in the *Daylight.* As 'one born not a great distance from the Point Pearce Mission Station' he wrote 'to express great sorrow in reference to the deplorable state of affairs in the Aboriginal Department'.[31] He revealed, his utter disgust that despite some 18,000 acres of good grazing land about Point Pearce and Wardang Island allotted 'for the benefit of the Aborigines',[32] the controlled and restrictive environment was not conducive to allowing Aboriginal success to generate. Echoing the same concerns as expressed by the AAPA leadership, Nurrunga Johnny rejected the Model Aboriginal State and was adamant that his people should be placed on land with which they were related. [33]

Support of Narrunga Johnny's position came from George Rankine, a remarkable self-taught Aboriginal man from Point McLeay Station who had been invited to provide evidence before the constitution commission. In that interview Rankine had declared 'What have the mission stations to show for 60 years of their existence — nothing!'.[34]

Another letter from Point Pearce, written by John Eustace Bews, carried similar powerful sentiments to those expressed by Narrunga Johnny, George Rankine and the AAPA members of New South Wales.

> The tenacity with which our governments adhere to the old time aboriginal law (called protection) of about 150 years ago is remarkable. Educated aborigines thoroughly understand its basic principles and know that it is this law that really matters because of its direct influence upon their every action. The deceptive policy miscalled 'protection'

does not protect and its continued practice spells destruction for the educated native ... we are under this unfortunate Act and classed as little children. [35]

Bews was himself a returned veteran of the First World War, one of many Aboriginal men who went off to fight for their country:

There have been Aborigines who have nobly responded to our Empire's "call to arms" overseas. Many have paid the supreme sacrifice ... we feel humiliated to know that we are still looked upon as a servile cringing race.[36]

George Rankine was not finished and once more wrote from the heart, and clearly stated where Aboriginal people were placed by white society:

We are not welcome in white society, and we do not wish to encroach upon it, but should be given the opportunity of living our lives in a community of our own. We shall then be able to show that we can produce industrials, scientists, poets and musicians just the same as the white man.[37]

The arguments put forth by these informed, articulate Aboriginal activists correspond unerringly to the demands delivered by Fred Maynard and the AAPA in New South Wales. They were calling for land to be made available to Aboriginal people and families, pointing out that land granted to Aboriginal people had been torn away and handed to white occupants, demanding that Aboriginal people should be placed in charge of their own affairs, and calling for the complete abolition of the present system of police and governmental control.

Around this time D Roper (father of the earlier cited Miss Roper, and former superintendent at Point McLeay for thirteen years) announced the formation of a new organisation to be called the Australian Aboriginal Association (AAA). Roper encouraged all Aboriginal people to join the association 'and have a voice'.[38] JC Genders, editor of the *Daylight*, added 'an Australian Aboriginals Association is in course of formation and it is hoped that it will affiliate with the Aborigines Protection League'.[39] It is surely more than coincidence that this organisation was formed and bore such a striking resemblance in platform to the AAPA. This same issue of the *Daylight* revealed further communication from the AAPA in New South Wales, and this correspondence is significant on a number of points, including demonstrating that the AAPA was still very active in late March 1928. It had elected a new secretary to replace Sid Ridgeway, and its planned newspaper *The Corroboree* was still in the pipeline. The letter to the *Daylight* reveals that the AAPA officers were instigating and encouraging a united national front to invoke governmental change to

Aboriginal administration. The letter, addressed to Genders and signed 'B Roundtree, Secretary AAPA', is reproduced in part below, with my emphasis added:

> Re the request of your Association for a *united front*, we say yes — our unswerving loyalty is with you, to *solidify the whole of the aboriginal position throughout Australia*, also for the abolition of the state control as constituted which we claim is against the best interest of our people.
>
> Re the copy of *"Daylight"* yes thanks delighted. Will extend greetings also your request for evidence Royal Constitution Commission in Sydney — all necessary information forthcoming. In conclusion our unswerving loyalty is with you for the emancipation of the aboriginal people in our own God given country. Our prayers are that reforms come quickly.'[40]

This issue of the *Daylight* also carried evidence of a growing national awareness and Aboriginal front opposing unjust government powers. William Harris of Morowa led an Aboriginal deputation, the 'Aboriginal Union', to political protest in Western Australia.

> A deputation of full-blooded aborigines and half-castes waited on the WA Premier (Mr Collier) to ventilate grievances in regard to the treatment of blacks. They appeared to be well educated. One is a vigneron in the Swan district and the others live around the metropolitan area. The Premier complimented them all on the logical way in which they placed their views before him. He assured them that he would give their case the utmost consideration.[41]

In early May the *Voice of the North* told an inspiring story of Aboriginal opposition to government policy and policy administrators, a story that bore a strong resemblance to that of Doris Pilkington — as portrayed in the acclaimed book and movie *The Rabbit Proof Fence*[42]:

> The Government of Western Australia has evidently perceived that public opinion is decidedly against their policy of dealing with the aboriginals. The case of the Jackson family has received wide publicity, and latest reports are to the effect that the Government has decided not to prosecute the father for taking possession of his children from the local authorities.[43]

The father's heroic and heart-rending efforts stand as a testament to the love and longing Aboriginal people held just as much as anyone else for their children. He apparently 'stole' his kids back and displayed inspiring courage and willpower, 'conveying four young children over one hundred miles of bush country in four days' in a feat that 'must excite the admiration and constitutes a complete refutation of the often repeated charge of a want of parental affection amongst the Australian native people'.[44]

The paper also reported Elizabeth McKenzie Hatton's return to Lismore, and described the successful AAPA campaign to place Aboriginal people on the state electoral roll. The subsequent impact on the recent election had drawn greater attention of state politicians, especially the 'Parliamentarian representatives on the northern rivers [who] have been particularly interested in the progress of the movement'.[45] The article conveys the success and inspiration that the AAPA and McKenzie Hatton had instigated:

> Two years ago the project was considered impracticable by most critics, but a few enthusiasts thought otherwise, and today they are witnessing results exceeding most ardent expectations. Once again is the fact made clear that the public generally will respond most liberally when any matter savouring of injustice is properly ventilated. The dignified persistence of Mrs Hatton secured for her mission the sympathy of people, police, preachers and politicians and Parliament will complete the good work in due course.[46]

In another development that undoubtedly held significance for the AAPA, Fred Maynard married Minnie Critchley — a white woman — at Darlinghurst on 14 June 1928.[47] There were long-held social barriers in place at the time to prevent such marriages, which were categorised by some as unthinkable, disgusting and to be discouraged at all costs. There has been and remains deeply entrenched stigma, stereotypes and taboo surrounding any understanding of relationships forming between Aboriginal men and white women both, historically and culturally.

One can only speculate upon the news of the Maynard–Critchley wedding in the wider public arena. At the time Maynard was the highest-profile Aboriginal political activist in the country, and now he had dared to cross the barrier of racial divide and marry a white woman! Minnie Critchley was not from a privileged background. Her family were English miners from Bolton, and they moved to the Hunter Valley to work in Newcastle and the coalfields. She was a single mother who worked in a coffee shop at Central Station in Sydney; indeed, Maynard met Minnie on a late night train. Her marriage to Fred Maynard resulted in Minnie being ostracised by her family but, as Shirley Maynard later reflected, 'Mum idolised dad'.[48]

Back in South Australia, the situation of the Ropers and the other residents of Point Pearce was distressing. Miss Roper sent letters to both the *Daylight* and the *Voice of the North*:

> Things are terrible here; they've taken 2/- a day off every married man's wages and are talking of taking another 1/- on Monday; single men are all off work and they are talking of putting off young married men. All

> the rations they give us is a quarter of a pound of tea, 2 lb sugar and 7lbs of flour and to tell you the truth … we are almost starving.[49]

The letter revealed the stupidity of those in control who denied the option of traditional sustenance for the community to harvest.

> Mr Johnson [the missionary] came down and gave us orders that we are not to catch a fish or spear a fish without a licence, only the full-bloods. He says we're not to catch them even for a feed, so how are we going to live? You can see for yourself how bad things are, even the animals are dying for food and the station itself is gone to ruins.[50]

After years of effort and boundless optimism, the frustration and anger felt by the Aboriginal political leaders and their supporters at the inaction of successive state and federal governments was displayed openly Dorothy Moloney, with venom in her words, targeted the Commonwealth government's reluctance to step forward in the wake of overwhelming evidence and take positive action: 'The most deplorable failure of the year and one that reflects adversely on the Australian nation as a whole, has been the neglect of the Federal Government to deal with the aboriginals of this continent. The same unfortunate conditions seem to prevail and the same cruel treatment has been chronicled with painful regularity'.[51] The majority of city dwelling people were still totally ignorant of the gross neglect of the Aboriginal population both in the past and the present; the old saying 'out of sight and out of mind' ruled the mindset of the masses.[52]

Moloney also targeted the state governments, whose neglect and blunt refusal to consider new methods or take advice on Aboriginal issues had resulted in extreme hardship, heartache and blatant oppression:

> The native people are long since extinct in Tasmania,[53] the Victorian Government has pressed its handful of aboriginals into the Station at Lake Tyres, whilst the Government of New South Wales is seemingly careless as to how soon the end comes. The South Australian Government has made a decent attempt to make good farmers of some of the aboriginals, but the great work remains to be done in Western Australia, the Northern Territory and Queensland.[54]

Dark economic clouds hung on the horizon, however, and they were to play a significant part in the slide from public view and into historical oblivion of Fred Maynard and the Australian Aboriginal Progressive Association. In what was to become a swansong for the *Voice of the North,* Dorothy Moloney directed attention once more to the neglect of governments to recognise the Aboriginal plight despite the economic downturn:

> The industrial crisis resulting from the position in the timber and coal trades has been responsible for the absorption of a large amount of time in the Federal and State Parliaments, and to such an extent as to prevent the case for the aborigines being properly presented or in any way fairly considered. The prevailing circumstances will, however, only mean a temporary postponement, for the reason that the people of Australia are determined to make amends for the tragedy which has besmirched the years which have passed since the advent of colonisation.[55]

Moloney unwittingly illustrated further evidence that there was also a new, detrimental voice on the horizon, one that would ultimately hold centre stage on Aboriginal issues and direction. That voice was the voice of white academia, and the AAPA and its supporters would ultimately be pushed to one side from the media platform by prominent white authorities such as AP Elkin and Michael Sawtell, both of whom were intent on promoting their own narrow views, profiles and positions of eminence. The proud Aboriginal political voice of the 1920s was to be drowned out and denied any opportunity to be heard as genuine spokesmen and women for their people or issues.

The *Voice of the North* survived the economic catastrophe of the Great Depression for a while, and even remained in publication until May 1933. However, its high-level exposure of the AAPA and its members was now over. The death of Dorothy Moloney in 1934 compounded the situation as, in her death, the Aboriginal community lost a great supporter and campaigner.[56] Despite the closure of the *Voice of the North* and the loss of his wife Elizabeth, John Moloney continued for the remainder of his life to campaign, speak out and write in favour of Aboriginal people and issues.

The Great Depression had a serious destabilising impact on the AAPA. They were Aboriginal men and women with families to care for, and their employment and financial standing was being seriously eroded. After their marriage the Maynards moved to Lakemba, and the Maynard children's memories of this very difficult period reveal the levels of hardship they endured. They recall the rented house with its long backyard where their father, Fred, grew his own vegetables. Minnie frequently walked from Lakemba to Bankstown for the 'relief', pushing her young son Mervyn (my father) in a stroller.[57] Despite the difficulties they had a wonderful home life. They always wore hand-me-downs, and Auntie Emma at Woolloomooloo helped clothe the kids once a year. 'Most of poor old mum's life was on handouts'.[58] They never had shoes that fitted. 'We had nothing to play with, no toys. Mervyn built his own boat from galvanised iron. We would pick the tar from the road on a hot day and fill the holes in the bottom of the boat'.[59]

Fred Maynard's working opportunities on the wharf evaporated. 'If you don't get called, you don't get work. If you didn't get the work you didn't get paid'.[60] Merv Maynard recalls going down to the wharf with his father. The kids would take a little empty box of Federal matches, and some of the men gave them half-pennies and pennies.[61] Fred Maynard queued and waited for work that never seemed to materialise. David Maynard commented that it appeared their father was always left out, but he didn't know if it was in response to Fred's political activities.[62]

The Maynards effectively went into hiding in their rented house at Lakemba and 'lived our own little reclusive life and dad protected us'.[63] It was freezing in the winter, 'dad put a blanket over us, followed by paper and a cow skin on top. He would heat a brick in the fire, wrap it in cloth and put it at the foot of the bed to keep our feet warm'.[64] Shirley Maynard recalled 'all through the night dad would come in and make sure I was tucked in'.[65]

The fact is that Fred Maynard was frightened. He was afraid to leave the children and his wife alone. Researcher David Huggonson revealed 'one can only speculate as to the threats that officers of the Board may have made in relation to taking Maynard's children into state care if he continued his agitation'.[66] This is corroborated through oral evidence of the Maynard children themselves, who indicate that threats were made against their father in relation to them. Merv Maynard recalled one horrifying account when, as a young boy, he was picked up along with another young Aboriginal boy and terrorised by the police at Canterbury police station. He recalled never having been so frightened. He was finger printed and the police proceeded to frighten the daylights out of him. He never said a word about the incident to his parents. Many years later he revealed:

> I never realised at the time, only being a bit of a kid, I didn't tell mum or dad for fear of getting into further trouble, but in retrospect the whole exercise had been about getting the point across to my father, that they could pick up and take us kids anytime they liked. Naturally they had expected me to relate the details to my father but I had just clammed up.[67]

This incident adds weight to the argument that police intimidation at the behest of the Board was at the forefront in initially forcing the Aboriginal leadership underground, and eventually forcing the total disintegration of the AAPA altogether. Certainly the evidence — dating back to 1924 when the Homebush Aboriginal girls' home set up by the AAPA was placed under police surveillance, and later through indications that material relating to the AAPA leaders had been gathered by authorities — adds weight to the possibilities of police interference and intimidation. The testimony of Bill Ferguson as noted by Jack Horner was that the AAPA was 'hounded out of existence by the police acting for the Board' tends to substantiate the theory.[68] During this period 'The *New South Wales Police News* encouraged policemen to look upon all radicals as their occupational enemies'.[69] Maynard's links to the trade union movement may have triggered further police aggravation directed towards him. The police were subjected to insidious propaganda that claimed that 'the only way of civilizing a "Red" [is] via the sawn off shot gun, the law of Judge Lynch, the rope and the baton. Friends! You will have to do that'.[70] Police culture at the time was permeated with such an ideology of right-wing extremes.

In spite of these attempts to intimidate Fred Maynard and frighten him away from his political activism, evidence indicates that he did not bow down. The AAPA had been driven underground, but was still in operation. The Maynard children recall visits to the home in Chullora of Sid and Cora Ridgeway (who had returned from Goulbourn) and their son Kevin. Sid was now working in the railway yards at Chullora, and the Maynard children remember playing around the Ridgeway place while the adults — their father, and uncles Dick Johnson, Sid Ridgeway and others — would sit in the kitchen discussing the political situation.[71] By the later 1930s Reuben Kelly was a young man working in Sydney, and he stated that the last time he heard Fred Maynard speak publicly was during this period in the grounds of the University of Sydney.[72] In the face of this evidence Maynard was still standing up, speaking out and refusing to be silenced on the rights of Aboriginal people, but he was keeping a weather eye to the heightened surveillance and public threats.

The Maynard children remember many visits with their father to La Perouse during the 1930s. There is little doubt that Maynard was still speaking out politically. This is corroborated with evidence of the La Perouse community's fight against revocation of their reserve. 'As early as 1926, Randwick Municipal Council had notified the Protection Board that it wanted the La Perouse reserve revoked and the residents moved'.[73] A site at Congwong Bay was selected by the Board, but the Aboriginal community resisted all efforts to remove them. In 1928 the residents of the community petitioned the New South Wales government.

The La Perouse community's fight for its reserve continued into the 1930s and, in a declaration of defiance and protest, the community declared its affiliation with the AAPA in its stance. The Aboriginal community's refusal to budge in the face of intimidation resulted in a deadlock. Eventually Randwick Council and the Board arrived at a compromise solution, which the reserve's residents were not party to and did not consent to. Under this agreement a portion of the reserve along the waterfront was revoked to become a public recreation reserve under Council control[74], but the Board was forced to greatly improve the homes at the reserve in accordance with council specifications. The Board's forced expenditure at La Perouse resulted in a great proportion of the Board's budget being absorbed there, resulting in Aboriginal housing of a vastly superior standard to any other reserve or station. [75]

But gains such as those at La Perouse were few, in spite of the fact that the Board continued to come under pressure and media scrutiny for its treatment of those people supposedly in its care. In late 1937 the Board attracted heavy media criticism over the callous and unfair manner in which Aboriginal people continued to be stripped of their land. A number of examples were cited, including the loss of the Mumbler and Linwood family farms on Fattorini Island over a decade before — losses which had been at the forefront of the rise of the AAPA.

One John B Steel wrote to the state premier, Bertram Stevens, incensed over reports published in the *Macleay Chronicle* on 7 July 1937. Steel stated that people everywhere were outraged at the callous treatment directed at the Aboriginal population. 'Some say why should the Aboriginals be turned off their reservations; they have a better claim to the land than the Government; THEY OWN THE LAND'.[76]

The arguments and evidence delivered were exactly the same as that powerfully delivered over a decade before with the AAPA. The Board, as it had done in the past, was quick to denounce and ridicule the claims made against it. They provided reports from police in the Macleay area stating that all of the claims were false and unsubstantiated. The sickening report delivered by the Board was full of deceit and attacked the Aboriginal landowners, describing them as being in debt and not having adequately kept their farms in order. These insidious accusations were in stark contrast to the facts, which reveal how successful for decades these Aboriginal farmers actually were. The Board in its conclusion wished to bury the revelations in the distant past and declared that its officer Donaldson, since deceased, would have cleared all of the incidents.

But the raising of these issues clearly demonstrates that Aboriginal people still carried deep and justified bitterness over their ill treatment. Only a month previously Percy Moseley, the son of Johnny Moseley, wrote to JJ Moloney and informed him of the Board and police being complicit in the demolition of Burnt Bridge.

The Manager of the AP Board came out on the 30th June and took possession of the place and took away the W.C. from the school. Father protested and asked him who had given him permission to remove the buildings and he said we had no right to question him. When he had gone with one load, we nailed up the fence and stopped him from coming in the second time, so he went in and brought the whole of the police force out to help him break the fence.

After they had broken down the fence and taken away the second load, the police, headed by the inspector, came down to the house and gave the Manager permission to take the tank off the place. Then I asked the Inspector what his duty was here, to which he replied, 'Give less cheek or I'll lock you up'.[77]

Aboriginal people had not forgotten or given up the fight or hope of justice. Johnny Moseley, now an old man, wrote an impassioned plea to the *Macleay Chronicle:*

Dear Sir,

Will you please find a corner in your paper for me please. I would like you to print this brief report in your paper. The Board has interfered with me and my property. They have taken the tank from my house: I protested and the Inspector of Police came out with the police force and issued orders for the manager of the Aborigines which has a station about a half a mile from me, to take the tank and anything he wanted. The manager broke down the fence, which was nailed and wired with barbed wire, and went in and took the WCs from the school. These things are all my property, so I maintain some rights to these buildings. I made a protest to the Inspector of Police and was told I owned nothing, that the Board owned everything; that I owned not even the land which I had spent the best part of my life working and improving for the past forty-five years. I thought I had fulfilled the conditions of the homestead leases. If these lands, which I claim, are converted into an Aboriginal reserve, I knew nothing about it. Now I ask is there any justice in that. If I had known these things long ago, while I had some strength left, I would have found residence elsewhere. Now it seems as if I have got to go and leave everything behind, my youth, my strength and nearly fifty years of hard labour. Oh Kempsey please help me. I have been a service to the state in my time. I have served my state with honesty. The very big thing I took pride in, the police force, two days ago made me feel as small as a slug under an elephant's foot. The state knows well of what service I refer to, when I was in the force as a black tracker, so I have no need to mention it here. I get a vote in the state and federal elections, so I appeal to the community for help.[78]

The tyrannical actions of both the Board and the police were cruel and malicious. One is left dumbfounded that the perpetrators of these crimes were left to declare themselves 'not guilty' of any crimes, and actually had the welfare of Aboriginal people at heart!

On the 24 November 1937, JJ Moloney sent a letter to the premier of New South Wales emphasising the importance of knowledgeable and capable people being able to present their case before the forthcoming commission into the role of the Board. It was the nucleus of the old guard of the AAPA that he pressed for inclusion in the commission, people like Elizabeth McKenzie Hatton and AAPA stalwart Johnny Donovan, 'a full-blood aboriginal who manages a timber mill in that district and who is a fluent advocate of the cause of his people'.[79] Others recommended by Moloney were Mr Flannery of Newcastle, who owned the timber mills at Booral and had intimate knowledge of the Karuah settlement, and the Rev. James Noble, 'a full-blood aboriginal'.[80]

Moloney also alerted the premier to the importance of 'another witness and very reliable man is Mr. Maynard, an aboriginal who resides at Lakemba'.[81] This revelation shows that Moloney had kept in touch with Fred Maynard in the intervening years and was aware that the AAPA president lived at Lakemba.

Despite Moloney's recommendation none of the AAPA members or its supporters was called or allowed to present evidence at the inquiry.

***

Sadly this effort by Moloney to once more try and instigate change in attitudes and policy towards Aboriginal people was to be his swan song: a month later he suddenly dropped dead in Sydney. His loss was a major blow to Aboriginal people. At the time of his death he was still valiantly taking up the fight on behalf of the Moseleys at Burnt Bridge.

The *Newcastle Morning Herald* gave coverage of what was a very large funeral for a much-revered local public figure. Mr R Weir President of the Australasian Society said of Moloney:

> [He] had a knowledge of Australian history that was little short of marvellous. This store of knowledge he had gathered after years of reading, travel and discussion. His efforts on behalf of the [A]borigines would be remembered with gratitude by the natives, whom he ever befriended ... None who sought his assistance ever sought in vain. He searched out injustice and fought manfully to have matters righted wherever this was found to be necessary. Newcastle has lost one of its most public spirited citizens — one who loved the land in which he was born, and spent his life in trying to further its interests.[82]

McKenzie Hatton continued to battle on and speak out in defence of Aboriginal people and issues. For her allegiance to Aboriginal people, McKenzie Hatton paid a price in the wider community. A woman now in her seventies, she still found the energy to appear in court and successfully assist in the defence of an Aboriginal man. Even decades after her experiences with the girls' home and the AAPA, she was still confronted by the levels of racism displayed against Aboriginal people. Describing the way the defendant and his supporters were treated, she remarked: 'I will not go into details of the sneering we received at the hands of the four or five solicitors present before the opening of the court'.[83]

But by the late 1930s and early 1940s her correspondence and comments reflect that she was disheartened, frustrated and disillusioned after being at the forefront of the fight for over two decades. Evidence from 1940 relays her desperate and emotional efforts to prevent 'a poor Aboriginal widow from being evicted from her home'.[84] McKenzie Hatton spent her later years in Queensland working with the South Sea Islander communities at Hervey Bay and Tweed Heads, and evidence of her contribution can be found in the records of the local historical society:

> Mrs Hatton lived in Coolangatta, circa 1935. Phyllis [Corowa] recalls that Elizabeth was in her eyes another 'Mother Teresa' working mainly with the South Sea Islanders. She became a 'Guardian' for many and assisted them when they were threatened with deportation, or had any money troubles.[85]

At the local level, Hatton continued to campaign for Aboriginal justice and rights until the end of her life, although she was never to regain her prominence in the national Aboriginal political fight. Despite all the heartache, opposition and hostility she had endured, reminiscences reveal that to the very end of her life she was a woman of great and unflinching faith. Carl Redman recalls McKenzie Hatton visiting his mother at their home at Cudgen: 'On one of her visits mum was concerned how Mrs Hatton would get home. Mrs Hatton replying "My father will provide for me", she walked out the door and stood at the curb and within minutes a car pulled over and she was offered a lift'.[86]

A week after the massive Allies' invasion of Normandy, Elizabeth McKenzie Hatton died, aged 73, on 13 June 1944. The local South Sea Islander community erected a large tombstone in her memory, with the inscription: 'Erected by the New Hebridians of the Tweed River in memory of their beloved missionary Elizabeth McKenzie Hatton'. As they had with JJ Moloney, Aboriginal people grieved a massive loss in her passing.

Fred Maynard, one of the last of the AAPA stalwarts, may have been driven underground but he did continue his political agitation — until 1944. In that year he was badly injured in what has been labelled a 'work-related accident'.[87] Fred was injured by what was described as large bails

A large gathering of predominately South Sea Islanders show their respects at the funeral for Elizabeth McKenzie Hatton. The memorial was built by the Islander community.

of compressed paper falling off pulleys at the wharf. However, when Fred's brother, Arthur, arrived at the Maynard home to deliver the news to Fred's wife, all that he said was, 'Minnie, Fred's had an accident and he's in the hospital. The leg is broken in six places, and don't expect any help from me'.[88] What sort of fear could drive his own brother to make such an announcement?

Family members doubt whether Fred Maynard's injuries were indeed the results of an accident. Kevin Ridgeway, the son of longtime friends Sid and Cora Ridgeway, was explicit on that point:

> Mum said till the day she died that what happened to Fredrick was no accident. It was all very fishy, hushed up, and no inquiry or investigation. She said Fredrick was very outspoken in a very dangerous time and they stopped him.[89]

There is little doubt that the activities of the AAPA and Fred Maynard had caused some deep concern within the power structures of both the New South Wales Aborigines Protection Board and the wider power base of Australian Government control. The chair of the Board was also the police commissioner, and that the police at that time had powerful links with the Sydney underworld is beyond dispute. However, Maynard had been out of the public political spotlight for more than a decade, surely this was far too long for some connecting thread of reprisal or silencing. Yet the oral testimony and family memory persists in the belief that there was something underhand in Maynard's hospitalisation.

Could it have been something to do with working on the Sydney docks — certainly a violent arena during those years? Maynard seemed to be forever overlooked for work, and perhaps it was his outspokenness on Aboriginal issues and working conditions that provoked some sort of violent reprisal. Or was it just an accident? The answer will probably never be solved.

Shirley Maynard recalled her father lying in hospital 'tied up to the ceiling in traction',[90] and the severity of his injuries would see him in and out of the hospital for the next twelve months. Although he returned to work, Shirley remembers him struggling home saying, 'I can't go to work. I have a sore foot, daughter'.[91] When she made him take off his shoes she found that 'it was up to his ankle and it was just black…it was gangrenous'.[92] Seriously ill, he was returned to hospital and his infected leg amputated.

Now there was no money for the family. To add to Fred's incapacity and suffering, he was diagnosed with what is now known as Type 2 diabetes, which can be brought on by physical and mental stress. 'We were the poorest family of all the kids who went to school. All of the other families had money — their fathers had jobs'.[93] The Maynards survived on charitable groups such as St Vincent de Paul, which 'fed the lot of us, every fortnight they gave us £3 it fed us'.[94]

Shirley Maynard vividly recalls going with her father, he on his crutches, 'to the eye hospital at St James' (his eye problems were probably linked to his diabetes):

> I never forgot that day. I just cried. It was so sad. We went through the Domain and came to a set of stairs to go down to the eye hospital and he fell from the top of the stairs to the bottom and I couldn't get him up'.[95]

Fred Maynard never recovered from the loss of his leg, his diabetes and the injuries he had sustained. His health continued to deteriorate and he died in Sydney on 9 September 1946.

In a fitting memorial his children look back with admiration. 'He must have had a great belief in his Aboriginal spirituality. You must have a driving power to get up and speak out'[96] and that Aboriginal people 'will never forget that side of our history … it is a scar that is being carried by all Aboriginal people'.[97]

9.
Conclusion

Great men, taken up in any way, are profitable company. We cannot look, however imperfectly, upon a great man without gaining something by him. He is the living fountain, which it is good and pleasant to be near. The light which enlightens, which has enlightened darkness of the world; and this not as a kindled lamp only, but rather as a natural luminary shining by the gift of heaven; a flouring light fountain, as I say of native original insight, of manhood and heroic nobleness; — in whose radiance all souls feel it is well with them. On any terms whatsoever, you will not grudge to wander in such a neighbourhood for a while.

Thomas Carlyle

This body of work has presented greater understanding of the rise of Aboriginal political activism and the prominent role Fred Maynard played in the movement. The Australian Aboriginal Progressive Association will be remembered as the first united all-Aboriginal political movement to mobilise in this country and take up the fight on behalf of Aboriginal people.

The methods they employed, particularly in recognising the importance of targeting widespread non-Indigenous support and their use of the media, were years ahead of their time. They clearly recognised that the key for Aboriginal people was land and their association to it, which was tied to defending and maintaining a strong cultural identity.

The international links and influences that impacted upon the AAPA most evident with Garveyism places an understanding of the rise on Aboriginal political protest well removed from the confines of national borders and historical understanding. One could argue that the AAPA did successfully slow the Board's policy of taking Aboriginal kids from their families — though perhaps this forced the Board to be more subversive in their raids. There is little doubt that the Board did play a role in the eventual disappearance and erasure of the AAPA and its memory. The AAPA tried valiantly to alter what it considered to be deliberate and detrimental government policies and actions that had serious and severe repercussions for Aboriginal people and issues. Sadly, many of these policies and actions continue to influence the thinking of many people in the wider Australian community today.

There can be little argument over the divide in equality between Black and white in Australia in the last century. Aboriginal peoples remain, by any socioeconomic or political standpoint, the most powerless and disadvantaged group in the country. In that respect history and historians — alongside the other major disciplines of anthropology, sociology and archaeology — have played a significant role in Aboriginal disadvantage. Aboriginal people have been depicted as a people without history, and have variously been described as noble savages, relics of the Stone Age, and as a dying race. Evidence surrounding the Aboriginal political fight of the 1920s, with the rise of the AAPA, boldly challenges many of these ingrained misconceptions of historical understanding.

Although the memory of the AAPA was forgotten, evidence reveals that many drew inspiration from its courageous stand — either directly or indirectly. To Burnum Burnum 'these were the Aboriginal pioneer activists who later became political role models ... They embodied a sense of human dignity and an indomitable strength of spirit, which were such an essential part of [my] inheritance'.[1] Pastor Frank Roberts was another great Aboriginal campaigner of the mid- to late-twentieth century whose family roots link to the AAPA struggle in the 1920s. The influence of the AAPA was clearly visible in his statements:

> In the past there were official policies, and even now there are pressures, that could lead to their extermination ... I feel it is important that the Aboriginal should be given freedom to take his place in society with the option of becoming part of the general Australian society, if he so desires...I think the Aborigines should be regarded not as people to be 'protected' ... The churches have tended to treat Aborigines as children.

Recently, Pat Dodson declared:

> We as Aboriginal people have got to stop looking at governments to keep giving us dough because that's how they co-opt us, that's how they divide us and that's how they corrupt us ... We have got to stop

being co-opted into the system because the more we do that the more we participate in our own demise'.[2]

It is amazing that, several decades earlier, the Aboriginal political leaders of the 1920s foresaw and were confronted with the very same insidious forces pitted against them. The AAPA and its supporters explained that the greatest obstacle facing the welfare of Aboriginal people was 'the system':

> [S]o long in vogue of handing out rations to the people and nursing them; these people were well able to work and support their own families and the AAPA was out to teach the people self-respect, and that could only be brought about when they took on the responsibility of their own support and development. [3]

The AAPA platform was unashamedly grounded in the collective good of Aboriginal people:

> It was progressive and aimed to lift the Aboriginal people in every way: spiritually, socially and industrially. It was an association, which suggested that they must pull together for the good of all'.[4]

More recently, Aboriginal commentator Bill Jonas (in his capacity as the Aboriginal and Torres Strait Islander Social Justice Commissioner) stressed:

> Citizenship rights alone are not enough. As a tool of social change they are inadequate and, indeed, entrench the inequality that already exists ... We need to go further with rights. We need to adopt a rights approach that does have the capacity to transform social, economic and political relations in Australia. We need to adopt social policies aimed at achieving equality, rather than assuming it; and we need to give full recognition to indigenous people's inherent rights, in particular native title. [5]

These very sentiments are echoes of Fred Maynard's inaugural address before 250 Aboriginal people assembled in conference in Sydney in 1925. Maynard said:

> We aim at the spiritual, political, industrial and social. We want to work out our own destiny. Our people have not had the courage to stand together in the past, but now we are united, and are determined to work for the preservation for all of those interests, which are near and dear to us.[6]

Recognition of the same call for 'political, social and industrial' reform several decades apart clearly outlines how little progress has genuinely been achieved. Evidence reveals that Aboriginal voices have for decades stated the obvious needs from an Aboriginal perspective, but if the past several decades are any indicator that voice will fall on deaf ears.

If this country is to attain any sense of maturity it must first of all deal with its past and come to terms with it and, through that process, provide a platform where both Black and white can walk together to a shared future of hope, prosperity and equality. Sadly, the whole debate has degenerated into an exercise of political and intellectual point scoring with little thought or compassion to the Aboriginal suffering in the past and the scars that impact and remain embedded in the Aboriginal psyche today. We have had to and continue to carry the psychological scars of this horrific period.

The very struggle of the AAPA symbolises the struggle of all minority groups around the globe who have been subjected not only to the physical and mental oppression of the time but also the historical remoulding and fabrication of events that distort and erase that memory. Overriding and breaking these long-established myths and misconceptions has never held greater importance.

Several decades after the Australian Aboriginal Progressive Association and its leaders were forced out of action, one is left to ponder and lament what might have been. If the AAPA's call for enough land for each and every Aboriginal family in the country had been met, we would have witnessed and reaped the benefits of several decades of Aboriginal people working productively and optimistically on their own independent and self-functioning areas of country. Similarly, if the AAPA demand that Aboriginal children were to be left with their own caring families, we would not have witnessed the horrific impact of a further five decades of horror and despair with thousands of Aboriginal kids being ripped away from their families. Finally, if a distinct rich Aboriginal cultural base and identity had been maintained we would not now be entwined in the slow process of putting together a giant fragmented jigsaw puzzle, with many of the cultural pieces — including stories and languages — missing completely. This country as a whole would have been so much the richer and embedded with a much clearer conscience of both its past and its future.

The present Australian historical climate is a clearly divided and politically charged environment of hostility. The great importance of revealing and recognising our erased histories is self-evident in any argument. Our histories can play a central role in exposing the hypocrisy and lack of historical credibility carried by those opposing their telling. The memory and legacy of Fred Maynard and the AAPA can inspire us on a path where prejudice, oppression, racism and inequality are fading memories of the past. Let us hope and dream of a future where all of our children of all backgrounds can join hands and walk together to a just, equitable and shared future of prosperity.

Bibliography

1. Unpublished archival material (non-government)

AP Elkin Papers, the University of Sydney.

Maynard family photographs and albums, courtesy of Cheryl Oakenfall, Dennis Maynard, David Maynard and Mary Kondek.

2. Records of historical societies and museums

Royal Australian Historical Society, Sydney.

Coffs Harbour Historical Society.

Dungog Historical Society.

Hervey Bay Historical Society.

Kempsey Historical Society.

Maclean Historical Society.

Newcastle Historical Society.

Scone Historical Society.

Tweed Heads Historical Society.

Wingham Historical Society.

3. Government archives

Australian Institute of Aboriginal and Torres Strait Islander Studies

Fletcher, J 1977, 'Transcript of an interview with New South Wales Aboriginal Protection Board Secretary Mr AC Petitt in June 1977', PMS 5380.

National Library of Australia

Australian Natives Association Journal, main reading room, Australian collection, N9 919.4005 ANA, vol. 1, no. 1 to vol. 3, no. 5 (7 December 1925 to 7 May 1928).

McKenzie Hatton, E 1918, *On Eagle's Wings,* Fitchett Bros, Melbourne.

McKenzie Hatton, E 1919, *How Can These Things Be?* Melbourne, Fitchett Bros.

McKenzie Hatton, E 1920s (exact date unknown), *Moluscut: stories of work amongst the sugar doodles of Queensland,* Sydney, R Dey.
Uplift, February 1941.

Victorian State Archives
Victorian Board for Protection Aborigines, correspondence, 10768 16, 8 January 1925.

Bills and Papers Office, Old Parliament House
Votes and Proceedings, House of Representatives 1926–28, vol. 1, pp. 691–4.

New South Wales State Archives
Archives Authority of New South Wales 1998, *A Guide to New South Wales State Archives relating to Aboriginal People,* p. 67.
Duren, J 1926, 'Letter sent to King George V', Box 5/14819, New South Wales State Archives, Sydney.
Governor-General's instruction to above, Box 5/14819, New South Wales State Archives, Sydney.
Maynard, F 1927a, 'Letter to the Premier', New South Wales Premier's Department, correspondence files, A27/915.
Maynard, F 1927b, 'Letter to Aboriginal girl', New South Wales Premier's Department, correspondence files, A27/915.
New South Wales Aborigines Protection Board, minute books, 1890–1901, 1905–06, 1911–69.
New South Wales Parliamentary Debates, 1905–1943.
New South Wales Aborigines Protection Board, reports, 1884–1939.
New South Wales Register of Aboriginal Reserves, 1875–1904.
New South Wales Premier's Department, correspondence files, A25/1742; A26/1251; A27/915.

Newcastle Regional Public Library
McKenzie-Hatton, E 1926, Newcastle Regional Public Library, Local Studies, Society of Patriots Archives.

National Archives of Australia
Australian Aboriginal Progressive Association, resolution AI/15 25/23976.
McKenzie Hatton, E 1918, National Archives, A2481 A1918/2962.
McKenzie Hatton, E 1921, National Archives, AI/15 21/6686.
McKenzie Hatton, E 1926, National Archives, A6680/1.
McKenzie Hatton, E 1926, National Archives, B741/3 V/3831.
National Archives of Australia, Relative to the issue of Certificate of Exemption in favour of Jack Johnson, memo no. 5934/08, D596.
National Archives of Australia, Register of departure of coloured persons from the Commonwealth, A38.
Suggested appointment of a Royal Commission on Natives (1927–1931) CRS A 659 1943/1/1451 (part 2).

New South Wales State Library (Mitchell Library)
Australian Aborigines Advocate, 1908–29, Q 572.9901/A.
Australian Inland Mission, correspondence and reports, MSS 7167, Box 1, minute books, Mitchell Library.
Our Aim: A Monthly Record of the Aborigines Inland Mission, 1923–61, MAV/ FM4/9719.
McKenzie Hatton, E to Retta Long, Aborigines Inland Mission, correspondence, donated by Christine Brett, uncatalogued, Mitchell Library.
Tetrin family notes on Melville House compiled through the Mitchell Library and the Maitland Historical Society.

South Australian State Library (Mortlock Library)
Retta Long, correspondence to Janet Mathews. Please note that this item is now missing.

Births, deaths and marriages
Registration of Births, Deaths and Marriages Act 1973 NSW, P90265/83 LC.
Registration of Births, Deaths and Marriages Act 1973 NSW, B 456214.
Registration of Births, Deaths and Marriages Act 1973 NSW, 7634 No 3302.
Registration of Births, Deaths and Marriages Act 1927 NSW, 016656.

4. United States of America Archives
The Negro World, Harvard University, University of California, Schomburg Centre for Research in Black Culture, Harlem, New York, NYPL.
The Crisis, Schomburg Centre for Research in Black Culture, Harlem, New York, NYPL.
Crusader, Schomburg Centre for Research in Black Culture, Harlem, New York, NYPL.
Journal of Negro History, Schomburg Centre for Research in Black Culture, Harlem, New York, NYPL.
Federal Surveillance of Afro-Americans 1917–25, 'The First World War, the Red Scare, and the Garvey Movement', 25 reels, A563, Lamont Library, Harvard University.
Clipping files 1925–74 (Australia) 000-384-1, Schomburg Centre for Research in Black Culture, Harlem, New York, NYPL.
Carter G. Woodson Files, Library of Congress, Washington DC, Reel 1, series 2, correspondence 1912–50.

5. Newspapers and periodicals
ABM Review, The Mission of the Church around the World, May/July 1973 vol. 63, no. 3.
Adelaide Advertiser 1920–28.
Bellinger and Nambucca Times 1924–28.
Bulletin 1906–08.

Coffs Harbour Advocate 1925–28.
Courier Mail (Brisbane).
Daily Express (London) 1910.
Daily Guardian 1924–28.
Daily Telegraph 1900—28.
Daylight (Adelaide) 1920–29.
Evening News 1906–27.
Grafton Daily Examiner 1924–28.
Herald (Melbourne).
Kyogle Advertiser 1919–28.
Macleay Argus 1919–40.
Macleay Chronicle 1924–40.
Macleay River Historical Society Journal.
Newcastle Chronicle 1869.
Newcastle Morning Herald 1900.
News (Adelaide).
Northern Star (Lismore) 1924–28.
Port Stephens Pilot 1925–27.
Referee 1906–09.
Register (Adelaide) 1925–27.
Sydney Morning Herald 1900–28.
Sydney Sportsman 1906–08.
Sun (Sydney) 1924–27.
Sunday Sun 1907.
Truth 1906–08.
Voice of the North 1920–30.
Walking Together.
Weekend Australian.
Wingham Chronicle and Manning River Observer 1900–28.

6. Oral interviews and testimonies, discussion and personal correspondence

Horner, J 1986, personal correspondence.
Horner, J 1996, personal conversation.
Maynard, J 1996a, oral interview with David Maynard, Mudgee.
Maynard, J 1996b, oral interview with Shirley Maynard at Woy Woy.
Maynard, J 1996c, oral interview with Mary Kondek at Toogoom.
Maynard, J 1996d, oral interview with Mervyn Maynard.
Maynard, J 1996–98, oral interviews with Reuben Kelly.
Maynard, J 1998, conversation with Kevin Ridgeway.
Maynard, J 1999–2001, oral interviews with Les Ridgeway.
Maynard, J 2000, oral interview with Vera Deacon at Newcastle.
Maynard, J no date, conversations with Peter Read, Heather Goodall, Carol Kendall and Geoff Gray.

Oakenfall, C 1987, personal correspondence to Jack Horner.

Maynard, J 2004, oral interviews with Pat Norris, Tom Norris and Joy Ross, grandchildren of Elizabeth McKenzie Hatton.

Maynard, J 27 September 1999, personal correspondence with Gwen Hart, research officer at the Lower Tweed Historical Society.

Maynard, J 22 July 2003, conversation with Carl Redman.

7. Published sources

Ackerman P and J Duvall 2000, *A Force More Powerful: A century of nonviolent conflict*, Palgrave, New York.

Baldwin, E, Longhurst, B, McCkraken, S, Ogborn, M and G Smith 2004, *Introducing Cultural Studies*, Pearson Education Ltd, Edinburgh.

Bennett, G [no date], *Early days of Port Stephens: Extracts from Sir Edward Parry's diary*, Dungog, Dungog Chronicle.

Blackburn, K 2002, 'Mapping Aboriginal nations: Nation concepts of late-nineteenth century anthropologists in Australia', *Aboriginal History*, vol. 26.

Blainey, G 1994, *The rush that never ended: A history of Australian mining*, Melbourne, Melbourne University Press.

Borrie, WD, Cuthbert, G, Wood, GL, Harris, HL and AP Elkin 1947, *A White Australia*, Australasian Publishing Company, Sydney.

Brown, D 1990, *Bury my Heart at Wounded Knee*, London, Vintage.

Chase, AK and JR von Sturmer 1973, '"Mental Man" and social evolutionary theory', in *The Psychology of Aboriginal Australians*, GD Kearney, PR de Lacey & GR Davidson (eds), Sydney, John Wiley & Sons, Australia.

Christiansen, J (1991), *They Came ... and Stayed: A history of Hervey Bay*, Hervey Bay, R & J McTaggart and Co.

Corris, P 1980, *Lords of the ring: A history of prize-fighting in Australia*, Cassell Australia Limited, North Ryde.

Davis, D 2001, *In the Image of God*, Yale University Press, United States.

Dawson, R 1831, *The Present State of Australia*, London, Smith Elder & Co.

Deacon, V 1992, 'Making do and lasting out', in *Depression Down Under*, Len Fox (ed.), Hale & Iremonger, Sydney.

Dos Passos, J 1961, *The 42nd parallel*, New York, Washington Square Press.

Fleischer, N [date unknown], *The Ring: Boxing the 20th Century*, The Ring, United States.

Fredrickson, G 1995, *Black Liberation: A comparative history of Black ideologies in the United States and South Africa*, Oxford University Press, New York.

Fryer, P 1984, *Staying Power the History of Black People in Britain*, Pluto Press, London.

Foley, G 1993, 'Assimilating the Mabo-Jumbo', in *Ngariaty — Kooris Talkin*, Bundoora, Victoria, La Trobe University Student Union.

Garvey, M 1970, 'Philosophy and opinions', in *Great Documents in Black American History*, George Ducas and Charles Van Doren (eds), Proeger Publishers, New York.

Gilbert, K 1994, *Because a White Man'll Never Do It*, Angus & Robertson, Sydney.

Goodall, H 1990, 'Land in our own country', *Aboriginal History*, vol. 14, Australian National University, Canberra.

Goodall, H 1996, *Invasion to Embassy: Land in Aboriginal politics in NSW, 1770–1972*, Allan & Unwin, St Leonards.

Goodall, H 2003, Evans Head History Report for the application for a native title determination, No. NG 6034, pp. 70–1.

Gray, S 1984, *Newcastle in the Great Depression*, Newcastle Region Public Library, Newcastle.

Griffiths, M 1995, *Aboriginal affairs: A short history 1788–1995*, Kangaroo Press, Sydney.

Harris, J 1990, *One Blood*, Albatross Books, Sydney.

Hartley D 1998, Lake Macquarie Memories, Fennel Bay, NSW.

Hill, R (ed) 1987, *Marcus Garvey: Life and lessons*, University of California, United States.

Hill, E 1995, *The Territory*, Sydney, Angus & Robertson.

Hinkson, M 2002, 'Exploring "Aboriginal" sites in Sydney: A shifting politics of place?', in *Aboriginal History*, vol. 26, 2002, Canberra.

Horner, J 1994, *Bill Ferguson: Fighter for Aboriginal Freedom*, self-published, Canberra.

Huggonson, D 1993, 'Aborigines and the aftermath of the Great War', in *Australian Aboriginal Studies*, no. 1, Canberra, AIATSIS.

Levine, LW 1993, *The Unpredictable Past: Explorations in American cultural history*, New York, Oxford University Press.

Martin, T 1976, *Race First*, Massachusetts, Majority Press.

Martin, T 1983, *Marcus Garvey, HERO*, Massachusetts, Majority Press.

Maynard, J 1997, 'Fred Maynard and the Australian Aboriginal Progressive Association (AAPA): One God, One Aim, One Destiny', *Aboriginal History*, vol. 21, Canberra.

Maynard, J 2001, 'Muloobinbah (Newcastle) an Aboriginal industrial Presence: Past and present', in *Journal of the Royal Australian Historical Society*, vol. 87, part 2.

Maynard, J 2005 'In the interests of our people. The influence of Garveyism on the rise of Australian Aboriginal political activism', in *Aboriginal History*, vol. 29.

Maynard, J 2007 'Circles in the sand. An Indigenous framework of historical practice', in *Australian Critical Race and Whiteness Studies Association Journal*.

Maynard-Kondek, M 1988, 'Charles Fredrick Maynard — Vision for Justice for Aborigines', in *Unsung Heroes and Heroines*, Suzy Baldwin (ed.), Victoria, Greenhouse Publications, as edited by Billy Marshall-Stoneking (author not recognised).

Malcolm X 1992, *The Final Speeches*, New York, Pathfinder.

Messner, A 2000, 'Popular constitutionalism and Chinese protest on the Victorian goldfields', in *Journal of Australian Colonial History*, vol. 2, no. 1.

Miller, J 1986, *Koori: A will to win*, Angus & Robertson, Sydney.

Moore, A 1989, *The Secret Army and the Premier*, New South Wales University Press, Sydney.

Morris, B 1985, 'Cultural domination and domestic dependence: The Dhangadi of New South Wales and the protection of the state', in *Canberra Anthropolgy*, vol. 8, nos. 1 & 2.

Morris, B 1989, *Domesticating Resistance: The Dhan Gadi Aborigines and the Australian State*, NSW, St Martins Press.

Mudrooroo 1990, 'Us mob and politics', in *Us Mob: History, Culture, Struggle: an Introduction to Indigenous Australia*, Sydney, Harper Collins.

Murphy, B 1982, *Dictionary of Australian History*, Sydney, Fontana/Collins.

Norst, M 1999, *Burnum Burnum*, Kangaroo Press, Sydney.

Pilkington, D 2001, *Rabbit-proof Fence*, St Lucia, University of Queensland.

Pryor, G 1988, 'Aboriginal Australians', in *Issues in Australian History*, R Willis, G Pryor, J Close and J Castle (eds), Longman Cheshire, Melbourne.

Unattributed 2000, 'Islands in the Macleay', *Macleay River Historical Society Journal*, no. 141, May.

Read, P 1996, *The Stolen Generations: The removal of Aboriginal children in New South Wales 1883 to 1969*, Sydney, NSW Department of Aboriginal Affairs.

Roe, M 1986, 'A model Aboriginal state', in *Aboriginal History*, vol. 10, nos. 1–2, Canberra.

Shoemaker, A 1992, *Black Words, White Page: Aboriginal Literature 1929–88*, Brisbane, University of Queensland Press.

Sommer, E 1998, *Marcus Garvey: The Forgotten Giant of Black Liberation*, <www.stewards.net/garvey.htm>, URL accessed 15 May 2000.

Turner, J and G Blyton 1995, *The Aboriginals of Lake Macquarie: A Brief History*, Newcastle, Lake Macquarie City Council.

Wells, G 1998, *Boxing Day: The Fight that Changed the World*, Harper Collins Publishers, Sydney.

Williams, V 1975, *The Years of Big Jim*, Lone Hand Press, Victoria Park, WA.

Willis, I 1994, 'Australian Aborigines Progressive Association', in *The Encyclopaedia of Aboriginal Australia*, D Horton (ed.), Aboriginal Studies Press, Canberra.

Willmot, E 1985, 'The dragon principle', in *Who Owns the Past?*, I McBride (ed.), Oxford University Press, Melbourne.

Willmott, E 1989, *The Inagural David Unaipon Lecture: Dilemma of Mind*, University of South Australia, Adelaide.

Wilson, J 1998, *The Earth Shall Weep*, Picador, London.

Wright, D 1992, *Looking Back: A History of the University of Newcastle*, University of Newcastle, Newcastle.

8. Theses and unpublished papers

Goodall, H 1982, 'A history of Aboriginal communities in NSW 1909–39', PhD, thesis, University of Sydney.

Hankins, C 1982, 'The missing links: cultural genocide through the abduction of female Aboriginal children from their families and their training for domestic service, 1983–1969', BA Hons thesis, University of New South Wales, Sydney.

Maynard, J 2003, 'Fred Maynard and the Awakening of Aboriginal Political Consciousness and Activism in Twentieth Century Australia', PhD thesis, University of Newcastle.

Notes

1. Introduction

1. Maynard, F 1927b, 'Letter to Aboriginal girl', NSW Premier's Department Correspondence Files' A27/915.
2. Pryor, G 1988, p. 412.
3. Malcolm X 2001, p. 71.
4. Malcolm X 2001, p. 71.
5. Shoemaker, A 1992, p. 24.
6. Shoemaker, A 1992, p. 23.
7. Willmot, E 1985, p. 46; Willmot, E 1991, p. 6.
8. Willmot, E 1985, p. 46; Willmot, E 1991, p. 6.
9. Booth, C and Tatz, C 2000, p. 12.
10. Goodall, H 1982, p. 13.
11. Goodall, H 1996, p. 236.
12. Horner, J 1994, p. 23.
13. Horner, J 1994, p. 27.
14. Horner, J 1986, p. 2.
15. Duren, J 1926, Box 5/14819, NSWSA.
16. Goodall, H 1996, p. 241.
17. Hinkson, M 2002, p. 71.
18. Goodall, H 1996, p. 24.2
19. *Wingham Chronicle and Manning River Observer*, 25 August 1925.
20. *Voice of the North*, 11 January 1926; Kooris is the term for Aboriginal people in the states of Victoria, Tasmania and most parts of New South Wales.
21. *Northern Star*, 3 August 1927.
22. Horner, J 1994, p. 26.

2. Fred Maynard's Early Years

1. Chase, AK and von Sturmer, JR 1973, p. 7.
2. *Newcastle Chronicle*, 13 November 1869.
3. *Registration of Births, Deaths and Marriages Act 1973* (NSW), P90265/83 LC.
4. *Sydney Morning Herald*, 23 October 1875.

5. *Sydney Morning Herald*, 23 October 1875.
6. *Sydney Morning Herald*, 23 October 1875.
7. Maynard, J 1996a, oral interview with David Maynard (Fred Maynard's son) at Mudgee. This quote and all others in this paragraph drawn from this source.
8. Maynard-Kondek, M 1988, p. 175. Mary Kondek-Maynard is Fred Maynard's daughter, and the author's auntie.
9. Miller, J 1986, pp. 126–27.
10. Goodall, H 1990, p. 23.
11. Goodall, H 1990, p. 116.
12. Goodall, H 1990, p. 80.
13. Maynard, J 1996b, oral interview with Shirley Maynard (Fred Maynard's daughter) at Woy Woy.
14. Messner, A 2000, p. 67.

3. Inspiration and Influences

1. Davis, D 2001, p. 95
2. Williams, V 1975, p. 31 (with thanks and appreciation to Arthur Shertock).
3. Maynard, J 2003, p. 95.
4. *The Crisis*, vol. 23, no. 3, January 1922.
5. *Daylight*, 31 August 1925, p. 920.
6. *Sydney Morning Herald*, 23 February 1904, p. 5.
7. *Sydney Morning Herald*, 23 February 1904, p. 10.
8. *Northern Daily Leader*, 5 September 1925.
9. *Daylight*, 31 July 1923, p. 618.
10. Fryer, P 1984, pp. 294–5.
11. Baldwin, E et al. 2004, p. 176.
12. Baldwin, E et al. 2004, p. 177.
13. Baldwin, E et al. 2004, p. 177.
14. *Sydney Sportsman,* 27 January 1907.
15. *Sydney Sportsman,* 27 January 1907.
16. *Sydney Sportsman,* 27 January 1907.
17. *Referee*, 30 January 1907
18. *Evening News*, 29 January 1907.
19. Wells, G 1998, pp. 44–6.
20. Wells, G 1998, pp. 44–6.
21. *Referee*, 13 March 1907.
22. *Referee*, 13 March 1907.
23. *Referee*, 13 March 1907.
24. *Truth,* 17 March 1907.
25. *Truth,* 17 March 1907.
26. *Truth,* 17 March 1907.
27. Maynard family photograph, courtesy Cheryl Oakenfall.
28. Willis, I 1994, p. 75.
29. Wells, G 1998, p. 178.
30. *Sydney Sportsman*, 20 March 1907.
31. *Sunday Sun,* 17 March 1907.

32. National Archives of Australia, Relative to the issue of Certificate of Exemption in favour of Jack Johnson, Memo No. 5934/08, D596.
33. Corris, P 1980, p. 93.
34. Corris, P 1980, p. 94.
35. Wells, G 1998, p.245.
36. Corris, P 1980, p. 94.
37. Corris, P 1980, p. 94.
38. Wells, G 1998, p. 197.
39. Wells, G 1998, p. 203.
40. See, for example, 'Race Riots in America, 19 deaths, many hurt and 5,000 arrested', *Daily Express* (London), 6 July 1910.
41. Recollections of Mr C.A. Henderson, 1864–1950, Mitchell Library MSS 1863, 7–734, quoted in Goodall, H 1998: 70–71
42. Martin, T 1983, p. 86.
43. Martin, T 1983, p. 86.
44. National Archives of Australia, Register of departure of coloured persons from the Commonwealth, A38.
45. Federal Surveillance of Afro-Americans 1917–25, The First World War, Red Scare and the Garvey Movement, Lamont Library, Harvard University, Index film A563.
46. Fredrickson, G 1995, p. 143.
47. Carter, G. Woodson Files 1912–50, Library of Congress, Washington DC, Reel 1, series 2, correspondence.
48. *Negro World,* 2 August, 1924.
49. Martin, T 1976, p. 93.
50. Davis, D 2001, p. 82.
51. Malcolm X, 2001, p. 71.
52. Martin, T 1983, p. 65.
53. Garvey, M 1970, p. 201.
54. Hill, R 1987, p. 327.
55. Levine, LW 1993, p. 132.
56. Martin, T 1983, p. 86.
57. Hill, R 1983 p. 495.
58. Martin, T 1983, p. 99.
59. Martin, T 1976, p. 42.
60. *Negro World,* 5 May 1923
61. *Negro World* 5 May 1923
62. *Negro World,* 5 May 1923
63. *Negro World,* 5 May 1923
64. Federal Surveillance of Afro-Americans 1917–25.
65. Hill, R 1985, p. 570
66. *Negro World,* 2 August 1924.
67. *Negro World,* 2 August 1924.
68. *Negro World,* 2 August 1924.
69. *Negro World,* 2 August 1924.
70. *Negro World,* 17 October 1925.
71. *Negro World,* 29 April 1922.

72. *Negro World,* 27 September 1924.
73. *Negro World,* 26 September 1925.
74. *Negro World,* 26 September 1925.
75. *Negro World,* 26 September 1925.
76. *Negro World,* 20 September 1924.
77. *Daylight,* 30 October 1924, p. 797.
78. *Bellinger and Nambucca Times,* 27 February 1925.
79. *Bellinger and Nambucca Times,* 27 February 1925.
80. *Adelaide Advertiser,* 18 April 1925.
81. Sommer, E 1998, p. 5.
82. Sommer, E 1998, p. 5.

4. Political Mobilisation

1. NSW Parliamentary Debates 1909, 4552.
2. NSW Parliamentary Debates 1911, Aborigines Protection Board, *Report 1910.*
3. NSW Parliamentary Debates, 1914–15, 1353.
4. NSW Parliamentary Debates, 1914–15, 1354.
5. NSW Parliamentary Debates, 1914–15, 1951.
6. NSW Parliamentary Debates, 1914–15, 1951.
7. NSW Parliamentary Debates, 1914–15, 1953.
8. NSW Parliamentary Debates, 1914–15, 1965.
9. Archives Authority of New South Wales 1998, p. 67.
10. Goodall, H 1996, p. 124. One Aboriginal soldier, George Kennedy, managed to secure a block at Yelta, within his own country to the south-east of Wilcannia.
11. Hankins, C 1982.
12. Maynard, J 2003, conversation with Carl Redman. Redman, born in 1930, is a member of the Tweed Heads region's South Sea Islander community. His father, Archie, and uncle, Otto, were the main instigators behind the memorial to McKenzie Hatton, donating £100 toward the construction. In recent years the memorial fell into disrepair, and Carl was responsible for its restored.
13. *Tweed Heads Daily News,* 6 June 1997, 'Historical Lookback' column by Peter Winter.
14. Maynard, J 2004, interview with Joy, Pat and Tom — grandchildren of Elizabeth McKenzie Hatton.
15. Maynard, J 2004, interview with Joy, Pat and Tom — grandchildren of Elizabeth McKenzie Hatton.
16. Christiansen, J 1991. Photos of McKenzie Hatton appear in this book with members of the Kanaka community on pages 115–16; she is erroneously referred to as 'Mrs Hutton'.
17. McKenzie Hatton, E 1921, National Archives AI/15 21/6686.
18. *Our Aim,* February 1909, p. 6.
19. McKenzie Hatton to Retta Long, Aborigines Inland Mission correspondence donated by Christine Brett, un-catalogued, Mitchell Library.
20. Maynard, J 2004.

21. National Archives of Australia, A2481, 1918/2962.
22. McKenzie Hatton, E 1918?, p. 1.
23. *Our Aim,* 20 March 1924, p. 12.
24. *The Herald* (Melbourne), 21 June 1921.
25. McKenzie Hatton, E 1921.
26. McKenzie Hatton, E 1921.
27. McKenzie Hatton, E 1921.
28. McKenzie Hatton, E 1921.
29. McKenzie Hatton, E 1921.
30. McKenzie Hatton, E 1921.
31. McKenzie Hatton, E 1921.
32. *Australian Aborigines Advocate*, 25 April 1921.
33. *Australian Aborigines Advocate*, 28 February 1918.
34. Miller, J 1985 p. 120–32.
35. *The Herald* (Melbourne) 21 June 1921.
36. *The Herald* (Melbourne) 21 June 1921.
37. *The Herald* (Melbourne) 21 June 1921.
38. *The Herald* (Melbourne) 21 June 1921.
39. *The Herald* (Melbourne) 21 June 1921.
40. *Our Aim*, 20 March 1924, p. 12.
41. AIM correspondence and reports MSS 7167, Box 1, Minute Books, 29 November 1923, Mitchell Library.
42. AIM correspondence and reports MSS 7167, Box 1, Minute Books, 10 January 1924, Mitchell Library.
43. AIM correspondence and reports MSS 7167, Box 1, Minute Books, 31 January 1924, Mitchell Library.
44. AIM correspondence and reports MSS 7167, Box 1, Minute Books, 31 January 1924, Mitchell Library.
45. *Our Aim*, 20 March 1924, p. 12.
46. *Our Aim*, 20 March 1924, p. 12.
47. AIM correspondence and reports MSS 7167, Box 1, Minute Books, 27 March 1924, Mitchell Library.
48. *Grafton Daily Examiner*, 29 December 1926.
49. Maynard, J 2003.
50. AIM correspondence and reports MSS 7167, Box 1, Minute Books, 4 September 1924, Mitchell Library.
51. AIM correspondence and reports MSS 7167, Box 1, Minute Books, 13 November 1924, Mitchell Library.
52. AIM correspondence and reports MSS 7167, Box 1, Minute Books, 11 December 1924, Mitchell Library.
53. AIM correspondence and reports MSS 7167, Box 1, Minute Books, 11 December 1924, Mitchell Library.
54. AIM correspondence and reports MSS 7167, Box 1, Minute Books, 11 December 1924, Mitchell Library.
55. AIM correspondence and reports MSS 7167, Box 1, Minute Books, 24 January 1925, Mitchell Library.

56. Victorian Board for Protection Aborigines, correspondence 10768 16, 8 January 1925.
57. New South Wales Aborigines Protection Board minute books, 23 January 1925, 4/7108–7127.
58. New South Wales Aborigines Protection Board minute books, 6 March 1925, 4/7108–7127.
59. *Our Aim*, 20 March 1925.
60. *Sydney Morning Herald*, 29 October 1924.
61. *Sydney Morning Herald*, 30 October 1924.
62. *Sydney Morning Herald*, 30 October 1924.
63. *Sydney Morning Herald*, 20 May 1922.
64. *Sydney Morning Herald*, 20 May 1922.
65. *Sydney Morning Herald*, 20 May 1922.
66. *Sydney Morning Herald*, 9 January 1925.
67. *Sydney Morning Herald*, 9 January 1925.
68. *Our Aim*, 20 December 1923.
69 *Voice of the North*, 10 December 1923
70. Wise, T 1985, p. 176.
71. Hartley, D 1998, p. 79.
72. Hartley, D 1998, p. 79.
73. *Voice of the North*, 10 November 1922.
74. *Daily Guardian*, 24 April 1925.
75. *Daily Guardian*, 24 April 1925.
76. *Daily Guardian*, 7 May 1925.
77. *Daily Guardian*, 7 May 1925.
78. *The Daily Guardian*, 7 May 1925.
79. *The Daily Guardian*, 24 April 1925.
80. *The Daily Guardian*, 24 April 1925.
81. *The Daily Guardian*, 24 April 1925.
82. *The Daily Guardian*, 24 April 1925.
83. *The Daily Guardian*, 24 April 1925.
84. *The Daily Guardian*, 24 April 1925.
85. *The Daily Guardian*, 24 April 1925.
86. Levine, LW 1993, p. 112.
87. Garvey, M 1970, p. 55.

5. The Rise and Impact of the 'Freedom Club'

1. New South Wales Aborigines Protection Board, minutes, 24 April 1925, 4/7108–7127.
2. New South Wales Aborigines Protection Board, minutes, 24 April 1925, 4/7108–7127.
3. New South Wales Aborigines Protection Board, minutes, 24 April 1925, 4/7108–7127.
4. New South Wales Aborigines Protection Board, minutes, 21 July 1925, 4/7108-7127.
5. *Macleay Chronicle*, 19 August 1925.
6. *Macleay Argus*, 7 April 1925.

7. *Macleay Argus,* 7 April 1925.

8. *Macleay Argus,* 7 April 1925.

9. *Macleay Argus,* 7 April 1925.

10. *Macleay Argus,* 7 April 1925.

11. Maynard, J 1996–98, oral interviews with Reuben Kelly, Uralla.

12. *Macleay Argus,* 7 April 1925.

13. *Macleay Argus,* 7 April 1925.

14. *Macleay Argus,* 7 April 1925.

15. *Macleay Argus,* 7 April 1925.

16. *Macleay Argus,* 7 April 1925.

17. *Macleay Argus,* 7 April 1925.

18. Garvey, 2003:164

19. *Australian Natives Association Journal,* 7 February 1926, p. 57.

20. Hill, R 1983, p. lxvi.

21. *Macleay Argus,* 7 April 1925.

22. The Island was named after Jean Baptiste Charles Lamonnerie Dit Fattorini, a French doctor who came to Port Macquarie in the early days of its settlement. As well as running his medical practice the doctor also established a timber-cutting operation on the island.

23. *Daily Guardian,* 2 May 1925.

24. *Daily Guardian,* 2 May 1925.

25. *Daily Guardian,* 2 May 1925.

26. *Daily Guardian,* 2 May 1925.

27. Goodall, H 1996, p. 123.

28. *Daily Guardian,* 9 May 1925.

29. *Daily Guardian,* 9 May 1925.

30. New South Wales Register of Aboriginal Reserves, 2/28349.

31. New South Wales Register of Aboriginal Reserves, 2/28349.

32. Telfer, E 1939, p. 54.

33. *Australian Aborigines Advocate*, Q 572.9901 A, Mitchell Library.

34. *Australian Aborigines Advocate,* 30 September 1915.

35. New South Wales Aborigines Protection Board, minutes, 11 September 1918, 4/7108-7127; Goodall, H 1982, p. 220.

36. Goodall, H 1996, p. 96.

37. Huggonson, D 1993, p. 7.

38. Morris, B 1985, p. 106.

39. Goodall, H 1988, p. 18.

40. Goodall, H 1990, p. 8.

41. *Coffs Harbour and Dorrigo Advocate,* 26 May 1926.

42. Goodall, H 1988, p. 6.

43. Morris, B 1985, p. 106; *Macleay Argus,* May 1925.

44. *Wingham Chronicle and Manning River Observer,* 10 June 1925; *Voice of the North*, 12 June 1925.

45. *Wingham Chronicle and Manning River Observer,* 10 June 1925; *Voice of the North*, 12 June 1925.

46. *Wingham Chronicle and Manning River Observer,* 10 June 1925; *Voice of the North*, 12 June 1925.

47. *Wingham Chronicle and Manning River Observer,* 10 June 1925; *Voice of the North*, 12 June 1925.
48. *Wingham Chronicle and Manning River Observer,* 10 June 1925; *Voice of the North*, 12 June 1925.
49. *Wingham Chronicle and Manning River Observer,* 10 June 1925; *Voice of the North*, 12 June 1925.
50. *Wingham Chronicle and Manning River Observer,* 10 June 1925; *Voice of the North*, 12 June 1925.original emphasis.
51. New South Wales Aborigines Protection Board, minutes, 13 and 20 June 1912, 4/7108–7127.
52. Goodall, H 1982, p. 224.
53. Morris, B 1985, p. 104.
54. *Daily Guardian,* 16 July 1925; *Wingham Chronicle and Manning River Observer,* 25 August 1925; *Macleay Argus*, 18 August 1925; *Macleay Chronicle*, 19 August 1925.
55. *Daily Guardian,* 16 July 1925.
56. *Macleay Chronicle* 19 August 1925.
57. *Daily Guardian,* 16 July 1925.
58. *Voice of the North,* 10 August 1925.
59. *Voice of the North,* 10 August 1925.
60. *Voice of the North,* 10 August 1925.
61. *Macleay Chronicle,* 19 August 1925.
62. *Daily Guardian,* 16 July 1925.
63. *Macleay Chronicle,* 18 August 1925.
64. *Macleay Argus,* 18 August 1925.
65. *Voice of the North,* 10 August 1925.
66. *Voice of the North,* 10 August 1925.
67. *Macleay Argus,* 18 August 1925.
68. *Macleay Argus,* 18 August 1925.
69. *Macleay Argus,* 19 August 1925
70. *Wingham Chronicle and Manning River Observer,* 25 August 1925.
71. *Wingham Chronicle and Manning River Observer,* 25 August 1925
72. *Wingham Chronicle and Manning River Observer,* 25 August 1925.
73. *Wingham Chronicle and Manning River Observer,* 25 August 1925.
74. *Wingham Chronicle and Manning River Observer,* 25 August 1925.
75. New South Wales Aborigines Protection Board, minutes, 23 October 1925, 4/7108–7127.
76. New South Wales Premier's Department, correspondence files, A26/1251.
77. New South Wales Premier's Department, correspondence files, A26/1251.
78. New South Wales Premier's Department, correspondence files, A25/1742.
79. New South Wales Aborigines Protection Board, minutes, 14 September1925, 4/7108–7127.
80. *Wingham Chronicle and Manning River Observer,* 10 November 1925.
81. *Australian Natives Association Journal,* 7 January 1926.
82. *Macleay Chronicle,* 7 October 1925.
83. Goodall, H 1996, pp. 152–3.
84. Goodall, H 1996, pp. 152–3.

85. Goodall, H 1996, pp. 152–3.
86. Maynard, J 1996b, oral interview with Shirley Maynard, Woy Woy.
87. Oakenfall, C 1987.
88. *Macleay Chronicle,* 7 October 1925.
89. *Macleay Chronicle,* 7 October 1925.
90. *Macleay Chronicle,* 7 October 1925.
91. Sommer, E 1998, internet article.
92. *Macleay Chronicle* 7 October 1925.
93. *Macleay Chronicle* 7 October 1925.
94. *Macleay Chronicle* 7 October 1925.
95. *Macleay Chronicle* 7 October 1925.
96. *Macleay Chronicle* 7 October 1925.
97. *Voice of the North,* 11 January 1926.
98. *Voice of the North,* 11 January 1926.
99. Australian Aboriginal Progressive Association resolution AI/15 25/23976, Australian Archives.
100. Australian Aboriginal Progressive Association resolution AI/15 25/23976, Australian Archives.
101. *Newcastle Morning Herald,* 1925.
102. New South Wales Aborigines Protection Board, minutes, 23 October 1925, 4/7108–7127.

6. A Year of Consolidation

1. *Wingham Chronicle and Manning River Observer,* 4 December 1925; *Voice of the North,* 10 November 1925.
2. *Voice of the North,* 10 December 1925.
3. *Voice of the North,* 10 December 1925.
4. *Voice of the North,* 10 December 1925.
5. *Voice of the North,* 10 December 1925.
6. *Voice of the North,* 10 December 1925.
7. *Voice of the North,* 10 December 1925, author's emphasis.
8. *Voice of the North,* 11 January 1926.
9. *Voice of the North,* 11 January 1926.
10. *Voice of the North,* 11 January 1926.
11. *Voice of the North,* 11 January 1926.
12. *Voice of the North,* 11 January 1926.
13. *Newcastle Morning Herald,* 10 February 1926.
14. *Newcastle Morning Herald,* 10 February 1926, author's emphasis.
15. *Newcastle Morning Herald,* 10 February 1926.
16. *Voice of the North,* 10 March 1926.
17. *Voice of the North,* 10 March 1926.
18. *Voice of the North,* 10 March 1926.
19. *Voice of the North,* 10 March 1926.
20. *Voice of the North,* 10 March 1926.
21. McGregor, R 1997, p. 118–19.
22. Aborigines Friends Association, papers SRG 139/1/65, Mortlock Library Adelaide, SA.

23. *Daylight*, 31 July 1926
24. *Negro World,* 17 October 1924.
25. Blackburn, K 1999, pp. 157–80.
26. *Voice of the North,* 10 May 1926.
27. See Brown, D 1990; Wilson, J 1998.
28. Register, 1 April 1925.
29. Register, 1 April 1925
30. *Advertiser* (Adelaide), 29 April 1925.
31. *Advertiser* (Adelaide), 29 April 1925.
32. *Register,* 1 April 1925.
33. *Voice of the North,* 10 June 1926.
34. *Daylight,* 30 September 1926.
35. *Daylight,* 30 September 1926.
36. *Daylight,* 30 September 1926.
37. *Sydney Morning Herald,* 15 November 1927; *Northern Star,* 19 November 1927.
38. Votes and Proceedings, House of Representatives 1926–28, vol. 1, pp. 691–4. My thanks to Mark Hargans and the staff at the Bills and Papers Office, Parliament House, Canberra.
39. *Sydney Morning Herald,* 24 March 1922
40. *Daylight* 30 October 1926.
41. *Daylight* 30 October 1926.
42. *Daylight* 30 October 1926.
43. *Daylight* 30 October 1926.
44. McKenzie Hatton, E 1926, correspondence to JJ Moloney, Society of Patriots Archives, Newcastle Regional Library. Original emphasis.
45. McKenzie Hatton, E 1926, correspondence to JJ Moloney, Society of Patriots Archives, Newcastle Regional Library.
46. *Macleay Argus,* 18 August 1925; Maynard, F 1927a, NSW Premier's Department, correspondence files A27/915; *Daylight,* 31 March 1928.
47. *Daily Guardian,* 24 April 1925.
48. New South Wales Aborigines Protection Board, minutes, 20 February 1930.
49. *Grafton Daily Examiner,* 22 December 1926
50. *The Grafton Daily Examiner,* 29 December 1926.
51. *The Grafton Daily Examiner,* 29 December 1926.
52. *The Grafton Daily Examiner,* 29 December 1926.
53. *The Grafton Daily Examiner,* 29 December 1926.
54. *The Grafton Daily Examiner,* 29 December 1926.
55. *The Grafton Daily Examiner,* 29 December 1926.
56. *The Grafton Daily Examiner,* 29 December 1926.
57. McKenzie Hatton, E 1926, correspondence to the Governor-General, National Archives A6680/1.
58. McKenzie Hatton, E 1926, correspondence to the Governor-General, National Archives A6680/1.
59. *Macleay Argus,* 24 February 1925.

7. 1927: The Struggle for Liberty

1. *Voice of the North,* 10 January 1927.
2. *Newcastle Morning Herald,* 25 March 1927.
3. *Newcastle Morning Herald,* 25 March 1927.
4. *Newcastle Morning Herald,* 25 March 1927.
5. *Voice of the North,* 11 April 1927.
6. *Voice of the North,* 11 April 1927.
7. *Voice of the North,* 11 April 1927.
8. New South Wales Aborigines Protection Board, minutes, 18 March 1927, 4/7108–7127.
9. *Voice of the North,* 10 May 1927; *Wingham Chronicle and Manning River Observer,* 3 June 1927; *Port Stephens Pilot,* 8 June 1927.
10. *Voice of the North,* 10 May 1927; *Wingham Chronicle and Manning River Observer,* 3 June 1927; *Port Stephens Pilot,* 8 June 1927.
11. *Voice of the North,* 10 May 1927.
12. *Voice of the North,* 10 May 1927.
13. *Voice of the North,* 10 May 1927.
14. Duren, J 1926.
15. Duren, J 1926.
16. Duren, J 1926.
17. *Voice of the North,* 10 June 1927.
18. *Voice of the North,* 10 June 1927.
19. *Voice of the North,* 10 June 1927.
20. New South Wales Premier's Department, correspondence files, A27/915; *Newcastle Morning Herald,* 2 July 1927; *Northern Star,* 6 July 1927.
21. *Australian Natives Association Journal,* 7 July 1927, p. 197.
22. New South Wales Premier's Department, correspondence files, A27/915; *Newcastle Morning Herald,* 2 July 1927; *Northern Star,* 6 July 1927.
23. New South Wales Premier's Department, correspondence files, A27/915; *Newcastle Morning Herald,* 2 July 1927; *Northern Star,* 6 July 1927.
24. *Voice of the North,* 11 July 1927.
25. *Voice of the North,* 11 July 1927.
26. *Voice of the North,* 11 July 1927.
27. *Voice of the North,* 11 July 1927.
28. *Voice of the North,* 11 July 1927.
29. New South Wales Premier's Department, correspondence from the under-secretary, 21 July 1927, PDCF 27/915.
30. Fletcher, J 1977, interview with AC Petitt [Pettitt in body of text].
31. *Northern Star,* 3 August 1927.
32. *Northern Star,* 3 August 1927.
33. *Northern Star,* 3 August 1927.
34. *Northern Star,* 3 August 1927.
35. *Voice of the North,* 10 August 1927; *Daylight,* 31 August 1927.
36. *Voice of the North,* 10 August 1927.
37. New South Wales Premier's Department, 2 September 1927, Aborigines Protection Board to the premier, PCDF, A27/915.

38. New South Wales Premier's Department, 2 September 1927, Aborigines Protection Board to the premier, PCDF, A27/915.
39. New South Wales Premier's Department, 2 September 1927, Aborigines Protection Board to the premier, PCDF, A27/915.
40. New South Wales Premier's Department, 2 September 1927, Aborigines Protection Board to the premier, PCDF, A27/915.
41. New South Wales Premier's Department, 2 September 1927, Aborigines Protection Board to the premier, PCDF, A27/915.
42. New South Wales Premier's Department, 2 September 1927, Aborigines Protection Board to the premier, PCDF, A27/915.
43. Maynard, F 1927a, New South Wales Premier's Department, correspondence files, A27/915.
44. Maynard, F 1927a, New South Wales Premier's Department, correspondence files, A27/915.
45. Maynard, F 1927a, New South Wales Premier's Department, correspondence files, A27/915.
46. Maynard, F 1927a, New South Wales Premier's Department, correspondence files, A27/915.
47. Maynard, F 1927a, New South Wales Premier's Department, correspondence files, A27/915.
48. Maynard, F 1927a, New South Wales Premier's Department, correspondence files, A27/915.
49. Maynard, F 1927a, New South Wales Premier's Department, correspondence files, A27/915.
50. New South Wales Premier's Department, correspondence files, A27/915.
51. New South Wales Premier's Department, correspondence files, A27/915.
52. *Voice of the North,* 10 October 1927.
53. *Voice of the North,* 10 October 1927.
54. *Voice of the North,* 10 October 1927.
55. Maynard, F 1927b, 'Letter to Aboriginal girl', New South Wales Premier's Department, correspondence files, A27/915.
56. Maynard, F 1927b, 'Letter to Aboriginal girl', New South Wales Premier's Department, correspondence files, A27/915.
57. Maynard, F 1927b, 'Letter to Aboriginal girl', New South Wales Premier's Department, correspondence files, A27/915.
58. Goodall, H 1996, p. 166.
59. New South Wales Premier's Department, correspondence files, A27/915.
60. Goodall, H 1996, p. 166.
61. Maynard, F 1927b, 'Letter to Aboriginal girl', New South Wales Premier's Department, correspondence files, A27/915.
62. Maynard, F 1927b, 'Letter to Aboriginal girl', New South Wales Premier's Department, correspondence files, A27/915.
63. Maynard, F 1927b, 'Letter to Aboriginal girl', New South Wales Premier's Department, correspondence files, A27/915.
64. Maynard, F 1927b, 'Letter to Aboriginal girl', New South Wales Premier's Department, correspondence files, A27/915.

65. Maynard, F 1927b, 'Letter to Aboriginal girl', New South Wales Premier's Department, correspondence files, A27/915.
66. *Voice of the North*, 10 November 1927.
67. *Voice of the North*, 10 November 1927.
68. *Evening News*, 14 November 1927.
69. *Sydney Morning Herald*, 15 November 1927.
70. *Sydney Morning Herald*, 15 November 1927.
71. *Sydney Morning Herald*, 15 November 1927.
72. *Sydney Morning Herald*, 15 November 1927.
73. Goodall, H 1996, p. 167.
74. *Sydney Morning Herald*, 15 November 1927.
75. *Sydney Morning Herald*, 15 November 1927.
76. *Sydney Morning Herald*, 15 November 1927.
77. *Sydney Morning Herald*, 15 November 1927.
78. *Sydney Morning Herald*, 15 November 1927.
79. *Sydney Morning Herald*, 15 November 1927.
80. *Sydney Morning Herald*, 15 November 1927.
81. *Sydney Morning Herald*, 15 November 1927.
82. *Sydney Morning Herald*, 15 November 1927.
83. Maynard-Kondek, M 1988, pp. 174–5.
84. Maynard-Kondek, M 1988, pp. 174–5.
85. Maynard, J 1996–98, oral interview with Reuben Kelly, Uralla.
86. Maynard, J 1996–98, oral interview with Reuben Kelly, Uralla.
87. Maynard, J 1996–98, oral interview with Reuben Kelly, Uralla.
88. *Sydney Morning Herald*, 15 November 1927.
89. *Northern Star*, 19 November 1927.
90. *Northern Star*, 19 November 1927.
91. *Northern Star*, 19 November 1927.
92. *Northern Star*, 19 November 1927.
93. *Northern Star*, 19 November 1927.
94. *Northern Star*, 19 November 1927.
95. *Northern Star*, 19 November 1927.
96. *Northern Star*, 19 November 1927.
97. *Grafton Daily Examiner*, 2 December 1927; *Northern Star*, 24 November 1927.
98. *Grafton Daily* Examiner, 2 December 1927.
99. *Voice of the North*, 12 December 1927.
100. *Voice of the North*, 12 December 1927.
101. *Voice of the North*, 12 December 1927.
102. *Voice of the North*, 12 December 1927.
103. *Voice of the North*, 12 December 1927.
104. *Grafton Daily Examiner*, 7 December 1927.
105. *Grafton Daily Examiner*, 10 December 1927.
106. *Grafton Daily Examiner*, 14 December 1927.
107. *Grafton Daily Examiner*, 24 December 1927.
108. *Grafton Daily Examiner*, 24 December 1927.

109. New South Wales Marriage Certificate 1927/016656; *Our Aim*, 23 January 1926.
110. New South Wales Premier's Department, correspondence files, A27/915.

8. The Final Curtain

1. Gilbert, K 1994, pp. 31–2.
2. Gilbert, K 1994, pp. 31–2.
3. *Voice of the North*, 10 January 1927; *Daylight*, 29 February 1928.
4. National Archives of Australia (Canberra), CRS A659/1, 1943/1/1451. Original capitals and elipses.
5. National Archives of Australia (Canberra), CRS A659/1, 1943/1/1451. Original capitals and elipses.
6. National Archives of Australia (Canberra), CRS A659/1, 1943/1/1451. Original capitals and elipses.
7. National Archives of Australia (Canberra), CRS A659/1, 1943/1/1451. Original capitals and elipses.
8. National Archives of Australia (Canberra), CRS A659/1, 1943/1/1451. Original capitals and elipses.
9. *Voice of the North*, 12 March 1928.
10. *Voice of the North*, 12 March 1928.
11. Maynard, J 1996–98, oral interview with Reuben Kelly, Uralla.
12. Maynard, J 1996–98, oral interview with Reuben Kelly, Uralla.
13. Maynard, J 1996–98, oral interview with Reuben Kelly, Uralla.
14. Gray, S 1984, p. 17; see Deacon, V 1992, pp. 95–120.
15. Maynard, J 2000, oral interview with Vera Deacon, Newcastle; Maynard, J 1999–2001, oral interview with Les Ridgeway, Bonny Hills.
16. Wright, D 1992, p. 84.
17. *Newcastle Morning Herald*, 12 July 1974.
18. *Newcastle Morning Herald*, 12 July 1974.
19. *Newcastle Morning Herald*, 12 July 1974.
20. Turner, J and Blyton, G 1995, p. 61.
21. Turner, J and Blyton, G 1995, p. 61.
22. Turner, J and Blyton, G 1995, p. 61.
23. *Walking Together*, no. 7, March 1994, p. 14.
24. *Walking Together*, no. 7, March 1994, p. 14.
25. *Voice of the North*, 12 March 1928.
26. *Voice of the North*, 12 March 1928.
27. *Voice of the North*, 10 April 1928.
28. *Daylight*, 31 December 1927.
29. *Daylight*, 31 December 1927.
30. *Daylight*, 31 December 1927.
31. *Daylight*, 31 January 1928.
32. *Daylight*, 31 January 1928.
33. *Daylight*, 31 January 1928.
34. *Daylight*, 28 February 1928.
35. *Daylight*, 28 February 1928.

36. *Daylight*, 28 February 1928.
37. *Dayligh.*, 31 March 1928.
38. *Daylight*, 28 February 1928.
39. *Daylight*, 31 March 1928.
40. *Daylight*, 31 March 1928, author's emphasis.
41. *Daylight*, 31 March 1928, author's emphasis.
42. Pilkington, D 2001.
43. *Voice of the North*, 10 May 1928.
44. *Voice of the North*, 10 May 1928.
45. *Voice of the North*, 10 May 1928.
46. *Voice of the North*, 10 May 1928.
47. New South Wales Certificate of Marriage, no. C 256922.
48. Maynard, J 1996b, oral interview with Shirley Maynard, Woy Woy.
49. *Voice of the North*, 10 July 1928.
50. *Voice of the North*, 10 July 1928.
51. *Voice of the North*, 10 December 1928.
52. *Voice of the North*, 10 December 1928.
53. This was a popular misconception of the period.
54. *Voice of the North*, 10 December 1928.
55. *Voice of the North*, 10 April 1929.
56. *Newcastle Morning Herald*, 27 December 1937.
57. Maynard, J 1996b, oral interview with Shirley Maynard, Woy Woy.
58. Maynard, J 1996b, oral interview with Shirley Maynard, Woy Woy.
59. Maynard, J 1996b, oral interview with Shirley Maynard, Woy Woy.
60. Maynard, J 1996a, oral interview with David Maynard, Mudgee.
61. Maynard, J 1996d, oral interview with Mervyn Maynard, Newcastle.
62. Maynard, J 1996a, oral interview with David Maynard, Mudgee.
63. Maynard, J 1996b, oral interview with Shirley Maynard, Woy Woy.
64. Maynard, J 1996b, oral interview with Shirley Maynard, Woy Woy.
65. Maynard, J 1996b, oral interview with Shirley Maynard, Woy Woy.
66. Huggonson, D 1993, p. 8.
67. Maynard, J 1996d, oral interview with Mervyn Maynard, Newcastle.
68. Horner, J 1994, p. 27.
69. Moore, A 1989, p. 86.
70. Moore, A 1989, p. 86.
71. Maynard, J 1996d, oral interview with Mervyn Maynard, Newcastle.
72. Maynard, J 1996–98, oral interviews with Reuben Kelly, Uralla.
73. Goodall, H 1996, p. 168.
74. Goodall, H 1982, p. 250.
75. Goodall, H 1982, p. 250.
76. New South Wales Premier's Department, correspondence files, 12/8749A.
77. New South Wales Premier's Department, correspondence files, A37/193.
78. *Macleay Chronicle*, 7 July 1937.
79. New South Wales Premier's Department, correspondence files, 12/8749A.
80. New South Wales Premier's Department, correspondence files, 12/8749A.
81. New South Wales Premier's Department, correspondence files, 12/8749A.

82. *Newcastle Morning Herald,* 28 December 1937.
83. *Uplift,* February 1941, National Library of Australia.
84. Maynard, J 28 December 1986, personal correspondence with Jack Horner.
85. Maynard, J 27 September 1999, personal correspondence with Gwen Hart, research officer at the Lower Tweed Historical Society.
86. Maynard, J 22 July 2003, conversation with Carl Redman.
87. Goodall, H 1996, p. 168.
88. Maynard, J 1996b, oral interview with Shirley Maynard, Woy Woy.
89. Maynard, J 1998, personal conversation with Kevin Ridgeway, Woolgoolga.
90. Maynard, J 1996b, oral interview with Shirley Maynard, Woy Woy.
91. Maynard, J 1996b, oral interview with Shirley Maynard, Woy Woy.
92. Maynard, J 1996b, oral interview with Shirley Maynard, Woy Woy.
93. Maynard, J 1996b, oral interview with Shirley Maynard, Woy Woy.
94. Maynard, J 1996b, oral interview with Shirley Maynard, Woy Woy.
95. Maynard, J 1996b, oral interview with Shirley Maynard, Woy Woy.
96. Maynard, J 1996a, oral interview with David Maynard, Mudgee.
97. Maynard, J 1996a, oral interview with David Maynard, Mudgee.

9. Conclusion

1. Norst, M 1999, p. 57.
2. *Weekend Australian,* 6–7 April 2002, p. 5.
3. *Macleay Argus,* 7 April 1925.
4. *Macleay Argus,* 7 April 1925.
5. *Australian,* 22 May 2002.
6. *Daily Guardian,* 7 May 1925.

Index